Spiritual Blessings from your Heavenly Father

Blessed be the God and Father of our Lord Jesus Christ, who has blessed us with all spiritual blessings in heavenly places in Christ (Ephesians 1:3)

James Glen Cox

Spiritual Blessings
from your
Heavenly Father

© James Glen Cox
2021

ISBN: 978-0-9966890-4-5

Soft Cover

All rights reserved.

No part of this book may be reproduced or transmitted in any form or by any means, electronic or mechanical, including photocopying, recording or by any information storage and retrieval system without permission in writing from the copyright owner.

Scripture references are from the
King James Bible for Today (KJBT, 2015).

HopeWay Publishers
Gate City, Virginia 24251
HopeWayBooks.com
hopewaybooks@gmail.com

Dedication

This book is dedicated to three people who impacted my life for eternity at the beginning of my spiritual life as a believer.

John Stuart Craft preached the Sunday night revival sermon when I was converted, June 7, 1964.

Rudene Kennedy ministered to young people in the churches in our area.

Robert Bryan was a missionary intern in a church in our community the summer I was saved.

John and Rudene have been promoted to their heavenly home.

Robert has been and still is an inspiration as he faithfully continues to serve the Lord.

Thanks

A special thanks to my wonderful wife Phyllis for her encouragement to write this book. Her help and suggestions through her editing skills have been invaluable.

Psalm 1

1 Blessed is the man who does not walk in the counsel of the ungodly, nor stands in the way of sinners, nor sits in the seat of the scornful.

2 But his delight is in the law of the Lord; and in his law does he meditate day and night.

3 And he shall be like a tree planted by the rivers of water, that brings forth his fruit in his season; his leaf also shall not wither; and whatever he does shall prosper.

4 The ungodly are not so: but are like the chaff which the wind drives away.

5 Therefore the ungodly shall not stand in the judgment, nor sinners in the congregation of the righteous.

6 For the Lord knows the way of the righteous: but the way of the ungodly shall perish. (KJBT)

Table of Contents

Preface		1
Introduction		3
Chapter 1	Redemption	7
Chapter 2	Forgiveness	21
Chapter 3	Holy and Without Blame	27
Chapter 4	Adoption	33
Chapter 5	Accepted	39
Chapter 6	An Inheritance	45
Chapter 7	Sealed with the Holy Spirit	53
Chapter 8	Enlightened	61
Chapter 9	Empowered	67
Chapter 10	Made Alive Spiritually	73
Chapter 11	God's Workmanship	79
Chapter 12	Made Near	87
Appendix A	Discussion Guide	93
Appendix B	About the KJBT	96
Appendix C	Ephesians – KJBT	97

Ephesians 1:2-3

2 Grace be to you, and peace, from God our Father, and from the Lord Jesus Christ.
3 Blessed be the God and Father of our Lord Jesus Christ, who has blessed us with all spiritual blessings in heavenly places in Christ. (KJBT)

II Peter 1:3-4

3 According as his divine power has given unto us all things that pertain unto life and godliness, through the knowledge of him who has called us to glory and virtue:
4 By which are given unto us exceedingly great and precious promises: that by these you might be partakers of the divine nature, having escaped the corruption that is in the world through lust. (KJBT)

Preface

Several years ago I came across a list of what all saints possess by being in Christ. The list was compiled by Arthur S. Leisching, missionary to Ceylon, who died in 1891. As I thought about his list, I reflected on my own observations. In over fifty years of being involved in various ministries, I have observed that many believers do not have any idea of all the blessings God has given to them as His children. Paul tells us in Ephesians 1:3 God "has blessed us with all spiritual blessings in heavenly places in Christ."

The goal of this project is to look at many of these spiritual blessings which are found throughout the New Testament. Many of these spiritual blessings are mentioned in the book of Ephesians. Each blessing will be presented in a brief devotional study. Hopefully, these studies will encourage the readers to dig deeper into the Word to learn more about each spiritual blessing which belongs to them. The goal is to help believers gain a better understanding of all God has given to them through their vital union with Christ.

Spiritual blessings are given to every believer for living in this present world. They provide the clarity which is necessary to face and deal with the chaos created by sin's curse. They are necessary in directing a believer's thinking so he may live each day with a biblical world view. These spiritual blessings are a constant source of enlightenment and encouragement. They give stability in the midst of the shifting sands of humanistic philosophy. They are a defense against the constant attacks and schemes of the evil one. These spiritual blessings keep one's attention focused on the things that last forever.

This is the first of several volumes which will present a number of spiritual blessings. Our Heavenly Father "has blessed us with all spiritual blessings in heavenly places in Christ" (Ephesians 1:3).

I want to present a disclaimer up front. I have been preaching for over fifty years. Some of the material presented may not be original because I may have read or heard it somewhere in those past fifty plus years. I will definitely give credit as well as the source for any statement if (a) I know who said it, (b) where I read it, or (c) where I heard it. If there is something I have heard or read, but do not know who said it or where I read it, I will simply acknowledge it is not original and add quotation marks.

The Scripture references in these studies are from the *King James Bible for Today,* 2015 (KJBT). The KJBT is the *Authorized King James Version* with the English updated from the last update which was in 1769 to the English language of today.

I published the *King James Bible for Today New Testament* in 2015. The KJBT is not a new translation. I updated the archaic words, spellings and endings of the old English. These changes simply make the *Authorized King James Version* much easier to read and understand for today's readers. You can read more about the KJBT in Appendix B.

The *Book of Ephesians* from the *King James Bible for Today* is Appendix C in this volume.

Introduction

The Epistle to the Ephesians has been called "The Heavenly Epistle." By many it is considered the most beautiful of all the Apostle Paul's writings. The great theme of the epistle is the relationship of the Church to Christ. This relationship is explained with a simple prepositional phrase which occurs over and over in the epistle. The phrase "in Christ," and other equivalent phrases are found in the epistle at least twenty-five times.

One must understand the Church is made up of individuals. It is neither a building, nor is the Church an organization. The Church is a living organism. It is the living body of Christ made up of individuals who have trusted Christ by faith for salvation. This salvation is a gift of God's grace to those who place their faith in Christ. Through saving faith, the believer has a vital or living union with Christ.

> For by grace are you saved through faith; and that not of yourselves: it is the gift of God: Not of works, lest any man should boast. (Ephesians 2:8-9)

> That if you shall confess with your mouth the Lord Jesus and shall believe in your heart that God has raised him from the dead, you shall be saved. For with the heart man believes unto righteousness and with the mouth confession is made unto salvation. (Romans 10:9-10)

When the Apostle Paul uses the phrase "in Christ," he is speaking of the vital union the individual believer has with the risen Christ. In this union, Christ takes the believer's sins and gives His righteousness to the believer. This vital union is a spiritual union in which the life of Christ becomes the spiritual life of the believer. Through the ministry of the Holy Spirit, Christ lives in the believer. In this union, Christ becomes the guiding Person in the believer's life. Paul makes it clear he understood Christ is the life of the believer.

> When Christ, who is our life, shall appear, then shall you also appear with him in glory. (Colossians 3:4)

> I am crucified with Christ: nevertheless I live; yet not I, but Christ lives in me: and the life which I now live in the flesh I live by faith in the Son of God, who loved me, and gave himself for me. (Galatians 2:20)

In this epistle, Paul shows the path from the absolute ruin of sin to the glorious provisions of redemption. This path leads from eternal death to eternal life in Christ. "And he has made you alive, who were dead in trespasses and sins" (Ephesians 2:1). God gives eternal life to the believer and then gives all spiritual blessings needed for his new life.

In Ephesians 1:1-2, the Apostle Paul introduces himself and addresses those to whom he is writing with his normal greeting of "grace and peace." In the very next verse, he shares the glorious truth God has provided a treasury of spiritual blessings for all believers.

> Paul, an apostle of Jesus Christ by the will of God, to the saints who are at Ephesus, and to the faithful in Christ Jesus: Grace be to you, and peace, from God our Father, and from the Lord Jesus Christ. Blessed be the God and Father of our Lord Jesus Christ, who has blessed us with all spiritual blessings in heavenly places in Christ. (Ephesians 1:1-3)

In verse three, Paul sets out four things about this tremendous treasury of spiritual blessings.

First, he declares these spiritual blessings are from God the Father of our Lord Jesus Christ. "The God and Father of our Lord Jesus Christ" is the believer's Heavenly Father who blesses the believer with all spiritual blessings. Believers bless their Heavenly Father with worship and praise, and He blesses believers with all spiritual blessings.

Second, he describes these blessings as being spiritual in nature. They are given and empowered by the Holy Spirit. These blessings deal with eternal things which enable the believer to follow Christ as he lives in this present world.

Third, he points out these blessing are brought to believers from Heaven and are heavenly in their import. Believers are enjoying some blessings now they will also enjoy forever in Heaven.

Finally, he explains all spiritual blessings for the believer have their source "in Christ." Only those who are in a vital union with Christ by faith will receive and experience these marvelous spiritual blessings.

At least twenty-one spiritual blessings are mentioned in the book of Ephesians. Others are found throughout the rest of the New Testament. These spiritual blessings can only be obtained and enjoyed through a personal faith relationship with Jesus Christ. Ephesians has six chapters which can be understood in two sections. Chapters 1-3 discuss the wealth of the believer and chapters 4-6 deal with the walk of the believer. The majority of spiritual blessings mentioned in the book of Ephesians are found in chapters 1-3.

The fall of humanity into sin was no surprise to God. His provision to deal with the fall into sin was not a reaction but rather a plan. God's great love for those who had been created in His image moved Him to provide for the catastrophic event of their fall into sin. The marred image is re-made "in Christ." Having been made a new creation, believers now have righteous standing before God. Salvation gives humans the same access to God which Adam possessed before his rebellion against God.

> For God so loved the world that he gave his only begotten Son that whoever believes in him should not perish but have everlasting life. (John 3:16)

> For whoever shall call upon the name of the Lord shall be saved. (I Corinthians 10:13)

Because believers are by faith in a vital union with Christ, they are chosen "in Him." All these spiritual blessings were foreordained to be given to those who by faith are in this vital union with Christ. Every spiritual blessing a believer receives or experiences in time or eternity is "in Christ."

The goal of this study is to share some of these spiritual blessings in order to help the believer better understand what he has "in Christ." Through these spiritual blessings, God gives the believer "all things that pertain unto life and godliness" (II Peter 1:3b). These are not in-depth theological studies. Rather, these are devotional thoughts which, hopefully, will encourage the reader to dig deeper into each spiritual blessing that belongs to every believer.

Not only are spiritual blessings found in the book of Ephesians, but they are also found throughout the New Testament. This study of spiritual blessings begins with those which are mentioned in the book of Ephesians.

Chapter 1
Redemption

> In whom **we have redemption** through his blood. (Ephesians 1:7a, KJBT)

All spiritual blessings from Heaven are eternal realities God has chosen to give believers because they are in a vital union with Christ. These spiritual blessings can neither be earned, achieved, nor purchased through human effort. These glorious blessings are given to those who are in Christ by faith out of the love and goodness of God.

Redemption is the foundational spiritual blessing which a believer has received through this vital union with Christ.

The word redemption or redeem has to do with liberation. Its basic meaning is "to buy back." The idea is to purchase in order to set free. In everyday use one could mean being set free from slavery, prison, captivity or any kind of bondage. The word redemption presupposes a bondage and need of deliverance. It means to purchase freedom by paying the required price in order to liberate. The one doing the redeeming must have the price sufficient to effect the liberation needed and a willingness to pay the price.

The word redemption can be used in reference to many different things. Something I remember from my youth illustrates this. My mother shopped at grocery stores which gave S&H Green stamps with purchases. When she had collected a sufficient number of stamps, we would all sit around the kitchen table and put them in the stamp collection books. We would lick stamps and stick them in the books until all the pages were filled. Those books of stamps could then be exchanged for various items listed in the S&H Catalog. She would need a certain number of books of stamps for a particular item. If she wanted to get a toaster, she would have to save the number of books of stamps listed in the catalog to get a toaster. The S&H Green Stamp Company had brick and mortar locations where she would take the books of stamps to get the toaster. Those locations were called "Stamp Redemption Centers." They were buying back their stamps with a toaster. The toaster was a sufficient price to redeem (buy back) and the books of stamps she possessed which had originally belonged to the S&H Green Stamp Company. They had liberated their stamps from my mom with the sufficient payment of the toaster.

There are three areas to which redemption is applied in the Old Testament. There are (a) the legal aspect (see Exodus 13:13; 34:20), (b) the relational aspect (see Leviticus 25:25-28 & 47-49 and Ruth 3:13; 4:1-6) and (c) the spiritual aspect which is to make atonement for sin by the providing the payment of an acceptable sacrifice. (see Leviticus where the phrase "make atonement" occurs many times). In all three areas, it is clear the idea expressed by redemption is setting free by the payment of a price.

The word in the New Testament which fits all three of these aspects of redemption is the word ransom. The concept of redemption or ransom predisposes bondage of some sort. The Jews understood this when Jesus promised them freedom.

> Then Jesus said to those Jews who believed on him, If you continue in my word, then you are my disciples indeed; And you shall know the truth and the truth shall make you free. (John 8:31-32)

The fact the Jews understood bondage was predisposed to being made free is demonstrated by their answer, "We are Abraham's seed and were never in bondage to any man: how can you say, You shall be made free?" (John 8:33). Jesus explained to them they were in spiritual bondage, "Truly, truly, I say unto you, Whoever commits sin is the servant of sin" (John 8:34). Jesus was telling them sin was their master and they were its slaves. He then promised He could free them from the bondage, "If the Son therefore shall make you free, you shall be free indeed" (John 8:36). Unless a person recognizes he is in bondage, he will never see the need to be liberated.

"But the Scripture has concluded all under sin" (Galatians 3:22a). Which means, all are under the bondage of sin. In the Book of Romans, chapters one through three, Paul lays out a clear and logical argument all are under the bondage of sin and therefore slaves to sin. Here is the conclusion of his argument.

> 9 What then? Are we better than they? No, in no way: for we have before proven both Jews and Gentiles, that they are all under sin;
> 10 As it is written, There is none righteous, no, not one:
> 11 There is no one who understands, there is no one who seeks after God.
> 12 They have all gone out of the way, they have together become unprofitable; there is no one who does good, no, not one.
> 13 Their throat is an open tomb; with their tongues they have used deceit; the poison of asps is under their lips:
> 14 Whose mouth is full of cursing and bitterness:
> 15 Their feet are swift to shed blood:
> 16 Destruction and misery are in their ways:
> 17 And the way of peace they have not known:
> 18 There is no fear of God before their eyes.
> 19 Now we know that whatever the law says, it says to those who are under the law: so that every

mouth may be stopped and the whole world may become guilty before God.
20 Therefore, by the deeds of the law there shall no flesh be justified in his sight: for by the law is the knowledge of sin.
21 But now the righteousness of God without the law is revealed, being witnessed by the law and the prophets;
22 Even the righteousness of God which is by faith in Jesus Christ unto all and upon all those who believe: for there is no difference:
23 For all have sinned and come short of the glory of God;
24 Being justified freely by his grace through the redemption that is in Christ Jesus:
25 Whom God has set forth to be a propitiation through faith in his blood, to declare his righteousness for the remission of sins that are past, through the forbearance of God.
(Romans 3:9-25)

Since, according to the Scripture every person is in bondage to sin, the only way for one to be liberated from this bondage is the payment of a price sufficient to purchase his freedom. This is the freedom from bondage to which Christ referred in John 8:36 when He said, "If the Son therefore shall make you free, you shall be free indeed."

Jesus tells us He came into this world to pay a sufficient price to liberate humans. "For even the Son of man did not come to be served, but to serve, and to give his life a ransom for many" (Mark 10:45). Note the word ransom which is the sufficient redemption price paid in order to liberate a person from slavery.

The Apostle Paul also uses the word ransom: "For there is one God and one mediator between God and men, the man Christ

Jesus; Who gave himself a ransom for all, to be testified in due time" (I Timothy 2:5-6). Christ gave himself a ransom for all because every person is under bondage to sin and needs to be set free from its condemnation, its penalty, and its power.

"For all have sinned and come short of the glory of God" (Romans 3:23). This verse is the conclusion of the argument presented in Romans chapters one through three. It declares all have sinned. "Truly, truly, I say unto you, Whoever commits sin is the servant of sin" (John 8:34). Since all have sinned, then all are servants or slaves to sin.

The conclusion is all humans are slaves of sin. However, believers in Christ have been delivered or set free from slavery. Faith in Christ is the only way one can be released from the bondage of sin.

> But give thanks to God that you were the servants of sin, but you have obeyed from the heart that form of doctrine which was delivered you. Having been made free from sin you became the servants of righteousness. (Romans 6:17-18)

Every person is also under the curse of or the bondage of the law. What is the curse of the law or the bondage of the law? The law demands absolute perfection in obedience to all the law of God. There is no provision in the law for a single failure in obeying the law. "For whoever shall keep the whole law, and yet offend in one point, he is guilty of all" (James 2:10). Since no one can live up to all the requirements of the law in its demand for perfection, everyone is condemned by the law. The law offers no remedy for human weakness and failure. This demand for absolute perfection leaves every human in a hopeless situation with no way to remove the guilt and condemnation for breaking the law. This hopeless situation is the curse of the law.

> For as many as are of the works of the law are under the curse: for it is written, Cursed is everyone who does not continue in all things which are written in the book of the law to do them. (Galatians 3:10)

God, however, has provided the solution to the perfection required by the law. He sent His Son into this world to pay the redemption price for humans. Christ fulfilled the law in every point while He lived upon the earth as a human. The perfect righteousness required by the law, which Christ accomplished as a man, has been given to everyone who is in Christ.

> Even so we, when we were children, were in bondage under the elementary principles of the world: But when the fullness of the time had come, God sent forth his Son, born of a woman, born under the law, To redeem those who were under the law, that we might receive the adoption of sons. (Galatians 4:3-5)

> For what the law could not do because it was weak through the flesh, God sending his own Son in the likeness of sinful flesh and for sin, condemned sin in the flesh: That the righteousness of the law might be fulfilled in us who do not walk after the flesh but after the Spirit. (Romans 8:3-4)

Humans also live their lives in bondage to death. This is another bondage which is common to every person on the earth. There are three types of death referenced in the Scriptures. They are (a) physical death, (b) spiritual death and (c) the second death.

> Forasmuch then as the children are partakers of flesh and blood, he also himself likewise took part

in the same; that through death he might destroy him who had the power of death, that is, the devil; And deliver those who through fear of death were all their lifetime subject to bondage.
(Hebrews 2:14-15)

Everyone is facing physical death as a consequence of the curse which came through Adam's sin. "And as it is appointed unto men once to die, but after this the judgment" (Hebrews 9:27). The eulogy for everyone who has ever lived is "and he died." "And all the days of Methuselah were nine hundred sixty and nine years: and he died" (Genesis 5:27). There are only two exceptions. Those were Enoch (Genesis 5:24) and Elijah (II Kings 2:1-12). Neither of them experienced physical death, for God took them directly. They have been the only two humans who have ever escaped physical death.

Ephesians 2:5 states the Ephesian believers had been dead in trespasses and sins before having been made alive by Christ. This statement is a reference to the fact all humans are spiritually dead. Spiritual death is the separation from and alienation from God while still being physically alive. When Adam sinned, he was immediately separated from God by spiritual death. When God warned Adam he "would surely die" in Genesis 3:17, He was not just talking about physical death, but the warning also included spiritual death. Spiritual death as well as physical death were passed on to all humans. "Therefore, as by one man sin entered into the world and death by sin; and so death passed upon all men for all have sinned" (Romans 5:12).

The Scriptures also reveal there is an everlasting death which is called the second death.

And death and hell were thrown into the lake of fire. This is the second death. (Revelation 20:14)

> But the fearful, and unbelieving, and the abominable, and murderers, and sexually immoral, and sorcerers, and idolaters, and all liars, shall have their part in the lake which burns with fire and brimstone: which is the second death.
> (Revelation 21:8)

Jesus refers this second death in Matthew's Gospel, "Then he shall also say unto them on the left hand, Depart from me, you cursed, into everlasting fire, prepared for the devil and his angels" (Matthew 25:41). This everlasting death is the eternal fate of those who die physically still being spiritually dead.

Christ liberates humans from every type of bondage by paying the redemption price. That price is His blood which He poured out on the cross of Calvary when He "gave His life as a ransom for many" (Mark 10:45).

> Who has delivered us from the power of darkness, and has translated us into the kingdom of his dear Son: In whom we have redemption through his blood, even the forgiveness of sins.
> (Colossians 1:13-14)

> For you know that you were not redeemed with corruptible things, like silver and gold, from your futile way of living received by tradition from your fathers; But with the precious blood of Christ, as of a lamb without blemish and without spot.
> (I Peter 1:18-19)

> Being justified freely by his grace through the redemption that is in Christ Jesus: Whom God has set forth to be a propitiation through faith in his blood, to declare his righteousness for the remission of sins that are past, through the

> forbearance of God; To declare, I say, at this time his righteousness: that he might be just and the justifier of him who believes in Jesus.
> (Romans 3:24-26)
>
> And they sang a new song, saying, You are worthy to take the scroll, and to open its seals: for you were slain, and have redeemed us to God by your blood out of every tribe, and tongue, and people, and nation; And have made us unto our God kings and priests: and we shall reign on the earth.
> (Revelation 5:9-10)

Christ has paid the ransom price to purchase believers for Himself. Those who put their faith in Christ to accept Him as Savior are His special purchased possessions. "For you are bought with a price: therefore glorify God in your body, and in your spirit, which are God's" (I Corinthians 6:20).

> But you are a chosen race, a royal priesthood, a holy nation, his own special people; that you should show forth the praises of him who has called you out of darkness into his marvelous light: Who in time past were not a people, but are now the people of God: who had not obtained mercy, but now have obtained mercy. (I Peter 1:9-10)
>
> Looking for that blessed hope, and the glorious appearing of the great God and our Savior Jesus Christ; Who gave himself for us, that he might redeem us from all iniquity, and purify unto himself a special people, zealous of good works.
> (Titus 2:14)

Included in the redemptive price is the redemption of the body as well as the soul.

> "For we know that the whole creation groans and travails in pain together until now. And not only they, but we ourselves also, who have the first fruits of the Spirit, even we ourselves groan within ourselves, waiting for the adoption which is the redemption of our body." (Romans 8:22-23)

Believers in Christ have been set free from the condemnation and control of sin. "For sin shall not have dominion over you: for you are not under the law but under grace" (Romans 6:14).

> There is, therefore, now no condemnation to those who are in Christ Jesus, who walk not after the flesh but after the Spirit. For the law of the Spirit of life in Christ Jesus has made me free from the law of sin and death. For what the law could not do because it was weak through the flesh, God sending his own Son in the likeness of sinful flesh and for sin, condemned sin in the flesh: That the righteousness of the law might be fulfilled in us who do not walk after the flesh but after the Spirit. (Romans 8:1-4)

Those who trust in Christ have also been liberated from the bondage of the law. Christ's perfect obedience to the law has been given to every person who has exercised saving faith in Christ. When a believer is viewed from God's perspective, he is seen as perfectly holy because he is seen in Christ

> Christ has redeemed us from the curse of the law, being made a curse for us: for it is written, Cursed is everyone who hangs on a tree: That the blessing of Abraham might come on the Gentiles through Jesus Christ; that we might receive the promise of the Spirit through faith. (Galatians 3:13-14)

> Knowing that a man is not justified by the works of the law, but by faith in Jesus Christ, even we have believed in Jesus Christ, that we might be justified by faith in Christ, and not by the works of the law: for by the works of the law shall no flesh be justified. (Galatians 2:16)

Spiritual death no longer holds sway over a believer. Believers are now spiritually alive in Christ. They live in communion and fellowship with the Creator of all which exists. "And you, being dead in your sins and the uncircumcision of your flesh, has he made alive together with him, ..." (Colossians 2:13).

> Knowing that Christ having been raised from the dead dies no more; death has no more dominion over him. For in that he died, he died unto sin once: but in that he lives, he lives unto God. Likewise also consider yourselves dead indeed unto sin but alive unto God through Jesus Christ our Lord. (Romans 6:9-11)

Physical death has been defeated by the hope of the resurrection. The body of flesh will die and decay, but that is not the end. The believer knows he will live forever.

> For this corruptible must put on incorruption, and this mortal must put on immortality. So when this corruptible shall have put on incorruption, and this mortal shall have put on immortality, then shall be brought to pass the saying that is written, Death is swallowed up in victory. O death, where is your sting? O grave, where is your victory? The sting of death is sin; and the strength of sin is the law. But thanks be to God, who gives us the victory through our Lord Jesus Christ. Therefore, my beloved brethren, be steadfast, unmovable, always

> abounding in the work of the Lord, forasmuch as you know that your labor is not in vain in the Lord. (I Corinthians 15:53-58)

Those who put their faith in Christ have no fear of the second death. "And these shall go away into everlasting punishment: but the righteous into life eternal." (Matthew 25:46) "Blessed and holy is he who has part in the first resurrection: on such the second death has no power, but they shall be priests of God and of Christ..." (Revelation 20:6).

Christ possesses the sufficient price for the redemption of every person who has ever lived or will ever live. The price is the blood of His sinless life.

> But Christ having come a high priest of good things to come, by a greater and more perfect tabernacle, not made with hands, that is to say, not of this creation; Not by the blood of goats and calves, but by his own blood he entered once into the holy place, having obtained eternal redemption for us. For if the blood of bulls and of goats, and the ashes of a heifer sprinkling the unclean, sanctifies to the purifying of the flesh: How much more shall the blood of Christ, who through the eternal Spirit offered himself without spot to God, purge your conscience from dead works to serve the living God? (Hebrews 9:11-14)

Christ not only possessed the sufficient price, but He was also willing to pay the price by laying down His life for all who would place their faith in Him.

> As the Father knows me, even so I know the Father: and I lay down my life for the sheep. And other sheep I have which are not of this fold: them I must

also bring, and they shall hear my voice; and there shall be one fold and one shepherd. Therefore does my Father love me, because I lay down my life that I might take it again. No man takes it from me but I lay it down of myself. I have power to lay it down and I have power to take it again. (John 10:15-18a)

Redemption is the foundational spiritual blessing. All other spiritual blessings come to a believer as a result of the restored relationship he has with God through the shed blood of Christ. God's redeeming grace liberates a believer from the guilt and condemnation of sin. It also sets a believer free from the bondage of the law and death. God sets the believer free to live the abundant life and to enjoy all the spiritual blessings He gives to every believer.

Psalm 51:1-15

*1 Have mercy upon me, O God, according to your lovingkindness: according unto the multitude of your tender mercies blot out my transgressions.
2 Wash me thoroughly from my iniquity, and cleanse me from my sin.
3 For I acknowledge my transgressions: and my sin is ever before me.
4 Against you, you only, have I sinned, and done this evil in your sight: that you might be justified when you speak, and be clear when you judge.
5 Behold, I was shaped in iniquity; and in sin did my mother conceive me.
6 Behold, you desire truth in the inward parts: and in the hidden part you shalt make me to know wisdom.
7 Purge me with hyssop, and I shall be clean: wash me, and I shall be whiter than snow.
8 Make me to hear joy and gladness; that the bones which you have broken may rejoice.
9 Hide your face from my sins, and blot out all mine iniquities.
10 Create in me a clean heart, O God; and renew a right spirit within me.
11 Cast me not away from your presence; and take not your holy spirit from me.
12 Restore unto me the joy of your salvation; and uphold me with your free spirit.
13 Then will I teach transgressors your ways; and sinners shall be converted unto you.
14 Deliver me from blood guiltiness, O God, God of my salvation: and my tongue shall sing aloud of your righteousness.
15 O Lord, open my lips; and my mouth shall show forth your praise. (KJBT)*

Chapter 2
Forgiveness

...the **forgiveness of sins**, according to the riches of his grace. (Ephesians 1:7b, KJBT)

Forgiveness further defines the totality of the liberty purchased by the blood of Christ discussed in the previous chapter on redemption. The importance of understanding forgiveness is shown by its addition to the definition of redemption as a separate blessing in Ephesians 1:7. Forgiveness is an integral part of redemption, yet it is given as a separate spiritual blessing. Without forgiveness one can neither stand in the presence of God, nor have any kind of positive relationship with God.

How is forgiveness to be understood? When one looks in a dictionary, one will find synonyms for forgiveness such as pardon, absolution, remittal, remission, exoneration, acquittal, etc. A believer needs to have a more developed understanding of the forgiveness of his sin than just synonyms from a dictionary.

The word used for forgiveness in Ephesians 1:17a means "a removal of" or "a getting rid of" or "a release from" something. In everyday use, it could be used in referring to a release from prison, getting rid of a debt, or the removing of anything which holds a person in bondage. The word forgiveness in this verse is clearly declaring redemption through faith in Christ has *completely removed* the sin of the believer.

There are several realities about this forgiveness which believers need to understand clearly. The first of these realities is when one puts faith in Christ, one's sins are covered. "And He is the covering for our sins: and not for ours only, but also for the sins of the whole world" (I John 2:2). Christ's blood covers the sin of every believer and is sufficient to cover the sin of all who will ever believe in Him. In the book of Romans, the Apostle Paul explains Christ is the propitiation for the believer's sin. The word propitiation means covering.

> Being justified freely by his grace through the redemption that is in Christ Jesus: Whom God has set forth to be a propitiation through faith in his blood, to declare his righteousness for the remission of sins that are past, through the forbearance of God; To declare, I say, at this time his righteousness: that he might be just and the justifier of him who believes in Jesus. (Romans 3:24-25)

> Even as David also describes the blessedness of the man unto whom God imputes righteousness without works, Saying, Blessed are they whose iniquities are forgiven and whose sins are covered. Blessed is the man to whom the Lord will not impute sin. (Romans 4:6-8)

The second reality of forgiveness for a believer is the condemnation of the law has been blotted out. Christ paid the penalty of sin for all believers. All humans are condemned. "Therefore, as by the offense of one judgment came upon all men to condemnation" (Romans 5:18a). Christ took on Himself the penalty of eternal death which resulted from this condemnation. Christ removed the condemnation and the penalty of sin from every believer by taking them on Himself and nailing them to His cross.

> And you, being dead in your sins and the uncircumcision of your flesh, has he made alive

> together with him, having forgiven you all trespasses; Blotting out the handwritten ordinance that was against us, which was contrary to us, and took it out of the way, nailing it to his cross. (Colossians 2:13-14)

The third reality of forgiveness is the blood of Christ cleanses the believer from all sin. "But if we walk in the light, as he is in the light, we have fellowship one with another, and the blood of Jesus Christ his Son cleanses us from all sin" (I John 1:7). All of a believer's sin has been washed away by the blood of Christ.

> And from Jesus Christ, who is the faithful witness, and the firstborn from the dead, and the prince of the kings of the earth. Unto Him who loved us, and washed us from our sins in His own blood." (Revelation 1:5)

This is the same message Isaiah had for Israel concerning its sin, "Come now, and let us reason together, says the LORD: though your sins be as scarlet, they shall be as white as snow; though they be red like crimson, they shall be as wool" (Isaiah 1:18).

The fourth reality of forgiveness is Christ has removed our sin. "And you know that he was manifested to take away our sins; and in him is no sin" (I John 3:5). The reason for which He came to earth was to remove sin from believers.

How complete is the removal of a believer's sin from the believer? The Psalmist expresses this reality, "As far as the east is from the west, so far has he removed our transgressions from us" (Psalm 103:12). He used east and west rather than north and south for a reason. If a person travels far enough north, he will eventually be traveling south. However, a person can travel east forever, and he will never end up traveling west. The Psalmist is portraying an infinite distance when says "as far as the east is from the west." Thus, there is an infinite distance to which the believer's transgressions have been removed from him.

The fifth reality of forgiveness is the wrath of God is no longer on the believer. The wrath of God abides on every unbeliever. Those who trust in Christ for salvation have been delivered from the wrath of God.

> He who believes on the Son has everlasting life and he who does not believe the Son shall not see life but the wrath of God abides on him. (John 3:36)

> And to wait for his Son from heaven, whom he raised from the dead, even Jesus, who delivered us from the wrath to come. (I Thessalonians 1:10)

> Much more then, being now justified by his blood, we shall be saved from wrath through him. (Romans 5:9)

The sixth reality of forgiveness is God will remember the believer's sin no more. "For I will be merciful to their unrighteousness, and their sins and their iniquities will I remember no more" (Hebrews 8:12). "And their sins and iniquities I will remember no more." (Hebrews 10:17). God tells us He is the One who can and will do this; "I, even I, am He that blots out your transgressions for my own sake, and will not remember your sins" (Isaiah 43:25). God in His sovereignty has chosen never to hold the believer's sin against him once it has been forgiven through the blood of Christ. That is His promise.

When there is an offense, which must be forgiven; the forgiving party must pay the price for the offence. Forgiveness is a gift the offended party gives to the offending party. The offended party must pay the full price of forgiveness in order to fully forgive. No payment, nor partial payment can be required. A debt which has been paid cannot be forgiven. No human can pay any part of his sin debt. God does not require, nor accept any payment. God is the offended party. All sin is against God. He has chosen to pay the full price of the forgiveness of sin by providing the full payment through the blood of Christ.

Forgiveness through the blood of Christ is the complete and total release from the guilt, condemnation, and penalty of sin because the debt has been paid by Christ. The penalty for sin which is eternal death has been satisfied. Sin's power over the believer has been broken. The believer is no longer under the wrath of God.

Having been forgiven, the believer also has the promise of escape from the very presence of sin when he leaves this world behind. The believer will spend eternity in Heaven worshipping his Heavenly Father.

The completeness of God's forgiveness flows from the abundance of His grace. How great is the grace of God? The Apostle Paul understood clearly the exceeding greatness of God's grace.

> And I thank Christ Jesus our Lord, who has enabled me, that he counted me faithful, putting me into the ministry; who was before a blasphemer, and a persecutor, and injurious: but I obtained mercy, because I did it ignorantly in unbelief. And the grace of our Lord was exceedingly abundant with faith and love which is in Christ Jesus. This is a faithful saying, and worthy of all acceptance that Christ Jesus came into the world to save sinners; of whom I am chief. (I Timothy 1:12-15)

The greatness of the gift of forgiveness can only be measured by the greatness of God's grace. Ephesians 1:7 declares the believer's forgiveness is "according to" the riches of His grace. It does not say "out of" the riches of His grace. Here is an illustration of the difference. A man who is a billionaire sees a need and gives $10,000.00 toward the need would be said to give "out of" his riches. If, however, the billionaire gave hundreds of millions of dollars to the need, he would be said to give "according to" his riches.

How rich in grace is God? Since God is infinite, there is no limit to His grace. His forgiveness is in accordance with His limitless supply of grace. God's forgiveness then is unlimited, sufficient, complete, and unchanging. The enormity of God's grace cannot be measured by any human method of measurement. However, every person who puts his faith in Christ experiences the infinite abundance of God's grace.

Humans have no claim to God's forgiveness, neither any power to compel God to forgive, nor any merit which could deserve forgiveness. Forgiveness is provided to believers according to the infinite wealth of God's grace. All one can do is receive this amazing gift of forgiveness through faith in Christ.

Once a debt has been forgiven, no further payment can be required because nothing is owed. One could say the believer's sin account has been stamped "**PAID IN FULL**" by the blood of Christ.

Chapter 3
Holy and Without Blame

> According as He has chosen us in Him before the foundation of the world, that we should be **holy and without blame** before Him in love.
> (Ephesians 1:4, KJBT)

There are two spiritual blessings to be discussed which are in this verse. God has chosen to give each of these spiritual blessings for all who are in Christ. These blessings are each believer is "holy and without blame before Him."

"Holy and without blame" could be said to be two sides of the same coin. Since they are almost synonymous, they will be discussed together in this chapter.

It appears "holy and without blame" were used in tandem for emphasis. The word "holy" approaches the blessing from a positive perspective; and the words "without blame," look at the blessing from a negative perspective. "Holy" is what has been given to those who are in Christ, and "without blame" states what has been removed from those who are in Christ. The words "before Him" give the position of this holiness and blamelessness. "Holy and without blame" is a declaration of the believer's standing before God.

The only way any human can approach God is by being completely holy. This means there must be a total and absolute absence of sin. Because of the inherent sin nature in humans, no one can attain the necessary holiness to approach God. "For all have sinned and come short of the glory of God" (Romans 3:23).

Even if it were possible for a person at some point to decide to live without sin and live a perfectly holy life from that point forward, he would still have to deal with his guilt of the sin before making his decision. There is no way for any person to remove the guilt for his own sin and make himself holy.

The only means by which any human may obtain the necessary holiness to stand before God is to receive holiness as a gift from God. This gift of the righteousness of Christ replaces all of the believer's sin with Christ's holiness. Those who are in Christ have been given the complete and absolute holiness of Christ. The Word of God reveals this righteous or holy position before God is a free gift. "Much more they who receive abundance of grace and of the gift of righteousness shall reign in life by one, Jesus Christ" (Romans 5:17).

Righteousness was imputed to Abraham by faith. In the same way righteousness is imputed to those who are in Christ by faith.

> He did not stagger at the promise of God through unbelief but was strong in faith, giving glory to God; And being fully persuaded that what He had promised He was able also to perform. And, therefore, it was imputed to him for righteousness. Now it was not written for his sake alone, that it was imputed to him; But for us also, to whom it shall be imputed if we believe on Him who raised up Jesus our Lord from the dead; Who was delivered for our offenses and was raised again for our justification. (Romans 4:20-25)

The word imputed means Christ's righteousness has been given to the person who trusts in Christ. Everyone in a vital relationship with Christ is now counted righteous or holy because of his faith in Christ. "And that you put on the new man, which after God is created in righteousness and true holiness" (Ephesians 4:24). Each believer has true holiness before God. It is true holiness because it is the holiness of Christ which has been given to the believer through his vital union with Christ. Believers are "partakers of His holiness" (Hebrews 12:10).

The other side of the coin is the phrase "without blame." God has given the believer holiness or righteousness and has simultaneously removed the guilt of sin thus making the believer "without blame." All are guilty because of their sin.

> As it is written, There is none righteous, no, not one: There is no one who understands, there is no one who seeks after God. They have all gone out of the way, they have together become unprofitable; there is no one who does good, no, not one. Their throat is an open tomb; with their tongues they have used deceit; the poison of asps is under their lips: Whose mouth is full of cursing and bitterness: Their feet are swift to shed blood: Destruction and misery are in their ways: And the way of peace they have not known: There is no fear of God before their eyes. Now we know that whatever the law says, it says to those who are under the law: so that every mouth may be stopped and the whole world may become guilty before God. (Romans 3:10-19)

In order for one to be blameless before God, this guilt must be removed. There is no way any human can remove his own guilt. God must remove the guilt in order for one to be blameless. God sent His Son to remove the guilt and condemnation of sin by taking the penalty for sin on Himself. Christ satisfied the penalty for sin on the cross for everyone who trusts in Him.

> For God did not send his Son into the world to condemn the world but that the world through him might be saved. He who believes on him is not condemned: but he who does not believe is

condemned already because he has not believed in the name of the only begotten Son of God. (John 3:17-18)

Christ is the only human to have ever lived without guilt or any blemish of sin. He was without sin. The Apostle John writes concerning Christ, "And you know that He was manifested to take away our sins; and in Him is no sin" (I John 3:5). Peter says Christ is "a lamb without blemish and without spot:" (I Peter 1:19). John the Baptist said to the crowd, "Behold the Lamb of God who takes away the sin of the world" (John 1:29).

Everyone who is in a vital union with Christ is blameless in his standing before God. The believer's position before God is the same as Christ's because Christ's righteousness has been given to every believer. The only acceptable standard with God is perfection. The only way any human can ever attain perfection is to possess the perfection of Christ. This perfection is received by faith in the death and resurrection of Christ. When God views the believer, what He sees is the perfection of Christ applied to the believer.

The believer's position of being "holy and without blame" is "before him." "Before him" emphasizes God's all-seeing eyes looking deep into the soul and searching the heart and mind. What He sees is the application of the righteousness of Christ to all who are in Christ by faith. God sees the perfect holiness of Christ applied to the believer and is well pleased with what He sees. Dr. Charles Sells explained it this way in his preaching, "In God's eyes, it is just as if a saved person had always been Jesus Christ."

The final words in Ephesians 1:4 are the words "in love." God loves those whom He created in His image. The original image has been marred by the curse of sin. Out of His love, God provides a solution for the marred image. Humans can be restored to position of "holy and without blame." "For God so loved the world that he gave his only begotten Son that whoever believes in him should not perish but have everlasting life" (John 3:16). When this verse uses the word "world", it is talking about all humans who live on this big ball of rock called earth.

The true believer now has a new desire which did not exist prior to his coming to faith in Christ. Pleasing God becomes the motivating goal of his life. Prior to salvation, one has no desire to please God and, in fact, cannot please God. "Because the carnal mind is enmity against God: for it is not subject to the law of God, neither indeed can be. So then they who are in the flesh cannot please God" (Romans 8:7-8).

Being "holy and without blame" before God will change the believer's character. His focus is to be on things which last forever, rather than the temporary things of this world. This focus will change the believer's total outlook on life. This concern about things which last forever will not only influence the believer's conduct and attitude immediately, but also will have an increasing influence on his conduct and attitude as he matures in his faith.

The book of Ephesians uses the illustration of changing clothes to explain the change in behavior. The believer is to put off the old self which is dominated by sin, and put on the new self which is dominated by the Holy Spirit. This process leads to conduct in line with the position of being "holy and without blame." This continuing change of conduct will come with study of the Word of God and the work of the Holy Spirit in the believer's life. Every aspect of the believer's life is to be directed by his being in Christ: homelife, work, church, pleasure, sports, personal relationships, associates, activities, attitudes, goals, and more. See Ephesians 4:17-5:20.

God gives all who are in Christ by faith the absolute holiness of Christ in their standing before Himself. God takes away all the guilt and condemnation of those who are in Christ as well.

Romans 8:1-15

1 There is, therefore, now no condemnation to those who are in Christ Jesus, who walk not after the flesh but after the Spirit.
2 For the law of the Spirit of life in Christ Jesus has made me free from the law of sin and death.
3 For what the law could not do because it was weak through the flesh, God sending his own Son in the likeness of sinful flesh and for sin, condemned sin in the flesh:
4 That the righteousness of the law might be fulfilled in us who do not walk after the flesh but after the Spirit.
5 For they who live according to the flesh do mind the things of the flesh; but they who live according to the Spirit the things of the Spirit.
6 For to be carnally minded is death but to be spiritually minded is life and peace.
7 Because the carnal mind is enmity against God: for it is not subject to the law of God, neither indeed can be.
8 So then they who are in the flesh cannot please God.
9 But you are not in the flesh but in the Spirit, if the Spirit of God dwells in you. Now if any man does not have the Spirit of Christ he is not his.
10 And if Christ is in you the body is dead because of sin; but the Spirit is life because of righteousness.
11 But if the Spirit of him who raised Jesus from the dead dwells in you; he who raised Christ from the dead shall also give life your mortal bodies by his Spirit who dwells in you.
12 Therefore, brethren, we are not debtors to the flesh, to live according to the flesh.
13 For if you live according to the flesh you shall die: but if you by the Spirit do put to death the deeds of the body you shall live.
14 For as many as are led by the Spirit of God, they are the children of God.
15 For you have not received the spirit of bondage again to fear; but you have received the Spirit of adoption, by whom, we cry, Abba, Father. (KJBT)

Chapter 4
Adoption

> Having predestinated us unto the **adoption of children** by Jesus Christ to Himself, according to the good pleasure of His will (Ephesians 1:5, KJBT)

Adoption is a legal action by which a person is voluntarily accepted and welcomed into a family. The adopted person receives all the benefits and privileges of the family into which he is adopted. A believer, because of his faith in Christ, is placed in God's family by a legal act of God. Every believer becomes a full-fledged son or daughter in God's family. "But as many as received Him to them he gave the authority to become the sons of God even to those who believe on His name" (John 1:12).

Adoption into the family of God is another of the spiritual blessings which belongs to all believers through their vital union with Christ. Those who were formerly "children of disobedience" and "were by nature the children of wrath" (Ephesian 2:3) have changed families. A believer has received the tremendous blessing of becoming an adopted child of God. The opportunity to be adopted into the family of God was provided when God sent His Son to the earth.

> But when the fullness of the time had come, God sent forth his Son, born of a woman, born under the law, To redeem those who were under the law, that we might receive the adoption of sons.
> (Galatians 4:4-5)

God determined ahead of time everyone who is in Christ by faith would receive the spiritual blessing of being adopted into

His family. Those who respond to the call of the Holy Spirit and choose to trust in Christ for salvation become members of the family of God. "Because all of you are the children of God by faith in Christ Jesus" (Galatians 3:26). As an adopted child, a believer has all the rights and privileges of a natural born child.

Those who are in Christ by faith have received the "Spirit of adoption." The Holy Spirit assures believers they are the children of God. It is through the ministry of the Holy Spirit in their lives believers are able to recognize God as their Heavenly Father.

> For as many as are led by the Spirit of God, they are the children of God. For you have not received the spirit of bondage again to fear; but you have received the Spirit of adoption, by whom, we cry, Abba, Father. (Romans 8:14-15)

Each believer can approach and speak directly to God from the vantage point of being His child. Jesus instructed His disciples to recognize God as their Father and to address Him as such in prayer. He wants to hear from His children.

> And it came to pass, that, as he was praying in a certain place, when he ceased, one of his disciples said unto him, Lord, teach us to pray, as John also taught his disciples. And he said unto them, When you pray, say, Our Father who is in heaven ...
> (Luke 11:1-2)

A believer's adoption is "by Jesus Christ." Spiritual adoption is through faith in what Christ has done. Christ came into this world as a human. He gave His life as a sacrificial death on the cross. He rose from the dead on the third day. Christ in His life, death and resurrection satisfied the justice of God against sin. A believer's faith in this finished work of Christ satisfies the justice of God against his sin. Having been cleansed from sin, made holy and without blame through faith in Christ, the believer is adopted into the family of God.

The believer's adoption is said to be "to Himself." Believers are brought into God's family by the authority of God Himself. God wants redeemed sinners to be members of His family. He made provision for sinners to become members of His family by giving His Son, Jesus Christ. Jesus Christ is God's "only begotten Son" (John 3:16). There are, however, multitudes of children in God's family. They are those who have been adopted into His family through several centuries since Christ arose from the dead. "For this cause I bow my knees unto the Father of our Lord Jesus Christ, From whom the whole family in heaven and earth is named" (Ephesians 3:14-15).

Why has God chosen to adopt those who trust in Christ into His family? The reason given is "according to the good pleasure of his will." His love moved Him to give this blessing to those who trust Christ as Savior. Adoption is not a blessing believers deserve, nor earn. It is what God does because He is good. God has chosen to adopt redeemed sinners because it brings Him great pleasure to bless those who trust in His Son. He wants believers to be in an intimate loving relationship with Himself. Thus, He has predetermined to adopt them into His own family.

Earthly fathers who love their children, do their very best to provide good and right things for their children. The believer's Heavenly Father loves His adopted children with an infinite love. Out of His love, He provides good things for His children. He knows what good things He wants His children to have and how to provide them.

> If you then, being evil, know how to give good gifts unto your children, how much more shall your Father who is in heaven give good things to those who ask Him? (Matthew 7:11)

> Every good gift and every perfect gift is from above, and comes down from the Father of lights, with whom is no variableness, neither shadow of turning. (James 1:17)

Believers can rest in the reality they are sons and daughters of the King of all the earth. The possibility of being adopted into the family of God emanates from God's great love for those whom He created in His own image.

> Behold, what manner of love the Father has bestowed upon us, that we should be called the sons of God: therefore, the world does not know us, because it did not know him. Beloved, now we are the sons of God, and it does not yet appear what we shall be: but we know that, when he shall appear, we shall be like him; for we shall see him as he is. And every man who has this hope in him purifies himself, even as he is pure. (I John 3:1-3)

As God's adopted children, believers are given instructions directly from their Father on how to live within the family of God. The children of the King should live in a way which brings honor and glory to the King.

> For the grace of God that brings salvation has appeared to all men, teaching us that, denying ungodliness and worldly lusts, we should live soberly, righteously, and godly, in this present world; looking for that blessed hope, and the glorious appearing of the great God and our Savior Jesus Christ; who gave himself for us, that he might redeem us from all iniquity, and purify unto himself a special people, zealous of good works.
> (Titus 2:11-14)

God wants His adopted children to be victorious in their spiritual lives. God will always lead his children to spiritual victory if they are willing to follow Him. "Now thanks be unto God, who always causes us to triumph in Christ" (II Corinthians 2:14a). It pleases the Father when His children are successful and triumphant in eternal matters.

The believer's Heavenly Father also corrects and disciplines His adopted children. The purpose of this correction is for the benefit of His children. Like any good father, God always wants what is best for His children. The believer's Heavenly Father is all-wise and all-knowing, so He always knows what is best for His child in the eternal scheme of things. God knows the things which last forever are best for His children. God's children too often just look at what is good for themselves today in this world, but God looks at what is best for them for eternity. The Heavenly Father only chastens those who are his children. God's chastening is proof one is a child of God. His chastening should not be looked at as punitive, but rather seen as loving correction.

> And you have forgotten the exhortation which speaks unto you as unto children, My son, do not despise the chastening of the Lord, nor faint when you are rebuked by him: For whom the Lord loves he chastens, and scourges every son whom he receives. If you endure chastening, God deals with you as with sons; for what son is he whom the father does not chasten? But if you are without chastisement, of which all are partakers, then you are illegitimate, and not sons. Furthermore we have had earthly fathers who corrected us, and we gave them respect: shall we not much more readily be in submission unto the Father of spirits, and live? For truly they chastened us after their own pleasure for a few days; but he for our profit, that we might be partakers of his holiness. Now no

chastening for the present seems to be joyous, but grievous: nevertheless afterward it yields the peaceable fruit of righteousness unto those who are trained by it (Hebrews 12:5-11).

A male child of a king is known as a prince and a female child of a king is known as a princess. Those are special and privileged titles in any kingdom. They are extra special titles in God's kingdom. These titles include all the wealth, position and responsibility which come with being children of the King of all the earth. As princes and princesses in the kingdom of God, believers are to live their lives in a manner which will never bring reproach to their Heavenly Father. The Father's honor should be paramount in the thoughts and actions of every one of His adopted children.

Chapter 5
Accepted

> To the praise of the glory of his grace, in which
> He has **made us accepted** in the beloved.
> (Ephesians 1:6, KJBT)

The first phrase in this verse, "to the praise of the glory of his grace," gives God's purpose in giving all spiritual blessings to His children. God has predetermined to give spiritual blessings to all those who are in Christ by faith. Spiritual blessings are not given for the believer's benefit, though they are a great benefit. Rather, spiritual blessings are given to bring praise to God for His glorious grace. Those who receive the spiritual blessings are to offer unending praise to "the God and Father of our Lord Jesus Christ." Knowing the source, provision, and purpose of spiritual blessings should result in continuous thanks and praise to the One who gave them. All God does and provides for believers originates in and proceeds from His glorious grace.

True praise and thanksgiving for His glorious grace can only ring forth from those who have experienced His saving grace. Grace is glorious in its nature, for it is a provision from the nature of a glorious God. Experiencing saving grace enables a believer to understand how wonderful the God who gives this glorious grace really is. Believers are to give thanks to God for what He does and praise Him for who He is. The more believers understand about the spiritual blessings which are theirs in Christ, the more vibrant their praise for their Heavenly Father should be.

One of the greatest desires of the human heart is the desire to be accepted. Humans will go to great lengths to do whatever they perceive as necessary to be accepted by others. There is a great longing for acceptance, approval and validation in every human heart.

Humans were originally created to be in fellowship and communion with God. They were created in God's image, perfectly acceptable, and thus were totally accepted by Him. They received their approval and validation from their Creator.

> And God said, Let us make man in our image, after our likeness: and let them have dominion over the fish of the sea, and over the fowl of the air, and over the cattle, and over all the earth, and over every creeping thing that creeps upon the earth. So God created man in his own image, in the image of God created he him; male and female created he them. (Genesis 1:26-27)

However, Adam sinned and brought sin into the human race. By his sin, Adam destroyed every human's acceptance with God. Sin also halted all human communion with God. The human position before God changed dramatically. Humans went from being completely accepted by God to being totally rejected by Him. The great human desire for acceptance by others may be the result of this rejection by God. Adam and Eve hoping to avoid God's presence when He came into the garden, covered themselves with leaves and hid among the trees. This reveals they realized immediately they were no longer perfectly acceptable to God. They no longer had any desire to commune with God.

> 6 And when the woman saw that the tree was good for food, and that it was pleasant to the eyes, and a tree to be desired to make one wise, she took of the fruit from it, and did eat, and gave also unto her husband with her; and he did eat.

7 And the eyes of them both were opened, and they knew that they were naked; and they sewed fig leaves together, and made themselves aprons.
8 And they heard the voice of the LORD God walking in the garden in the cool of the day: and Adam and his wife hid themselves from the presence of the LORD God among the trees of the garden.
9 And the LORD God called unto Adam, and said unto him, Where are you?
10 And he said, I heard your voice in the garden, and I was afraid, because I was naked; and I hid myself.
11 And he said, Who told you that you were naked? Have you eaten of the tree, of which I commanded you that you should not eat? (Genesis 3:6-11)

So, it seems humans having been rejected by God, seek acceptance and validation from other humans to replace the loss of their divine acceptance.

Many seek to renew their acceptance with God through various religions, rituals, good deeds, religious activities, giving, sacrificing, etc. Religion is one of the most universal aspects of human culture. The Museum of Natural History at the Smithsonian Institute in Washington, D.C. has a display of what historians presume a caveman encampment would look like. In the midst their display is a symbol a of some sort of religion. Every culture, no matter how primitive or advanced, has some type of religious belief.

The need for acceptance is so great in humans they will go to great lengths in their efforts to restore their position of being accepted by God. There, however, is nothing anyone can do by himself or for himself in order to become acceptable to God. Sin makes every human totally unacceptable to God. No human by his own effort can restore perfect acceptance by God which originally existed. There is no possible way any human can pay for his own sin.

> Knowing that a man is not justified by the works of the law, but by faith in Jesus Christ, even we have believed in Jesus Christ, that we might be justified by faith in Christ, and not by the works of the law: for by the works of the law shall no flesh be justified. (Galatians 2:16)

Thankfully, however, it is possible for a human to return to the position of being perfectly acceptable to God and being totally accepted by Him. This change of position can only be accomplished by an act of God on their behalf. Ephesians 1:6 says God has "made us accepted." God has made the believer acceptable by recreating him spiritually. It is a change which God has made in a believer no one could ever do for himself. By His grace, God provides the means for humans to go from absolute rejection back to complete acceptance before Himself. The way back to this total acceptance by God is through faith in Christ.

> But after that the kindness and love of God our Savior toward man appeared, Not by works of righteousness which we have done, but according to his mercy he saved us, by the washing of regeneration, and renewing of the Holy Spirit; Which he shed on us abundantly through Jesus Christ our Savior; That being justified by his grace, we should be made heirs according to the hope of eternal life. (Titus 3:4-7)

The means whereby God provides this total acceptance is "in the Beloved." The Beloved in Ephesians 1:6 is the only begotten Son of God who is the Beloved of the Father. Jesus is the Son whom the Father loves with a perfect and eternal love.

> And Jesus, when he was baptized, went up immediately out of the water: and, lo, the heavens were opened unto him, and he saw the Spirit of God descending like a dove, and lighting upon him: And lo a voice from heaven, saying, This is my beloved Son, in whom I am well pleased."
> (Matthew 3:16-17)

The little preposition "in" is very significant when it appears before Christ. It refers to the vital union a believer has with Christ through his faith in the death and resurrection of Christ. "That if you shall confess with your mouth the Lord Jesus, and shall believe in your heart that God has raised him from the dead, you shall be saved" (Romans 10:9). Through this vital union, a believer has been made into a new person spiritually. "Therefore if any man is in Christ, he is a new creation: old things have passed away; behold, all things have become new" (II Corinthians 5:17).

By being in Christ and having been made a new creation, the believers have been made acceptable to God and is accepted by Him. This new position for the believers of being made acceptable and being accepted is an act of God's glorious grace. Through faith in Christ, one goes from absolute rejection by God to complete acceptance before God. In spite of all their failures, fears, inconsistencies, weaknesses, problems and sin, those in Christ are fully accepted by God. God's acceptance of a person is neither based on anything a person is, nor what a person does. Rather, acceptance is a gift based on the outpouring of God's glorious grace. Believers are as accepted before God as Christ Himself because they are in the Beloved. The late, great radio preacher J. Vernon McGee declared, "God sees the believer in Christ; and He accepts the believer, just as He receives His own Son."

Believers are absolutely accepted in Christ. Through God's glorious grace, believers now meet all the righteous requirements of the law. They have been given all of the absolute righteousness of Christ. By being in Christ, the believer has met every demand of the law. Christ fulfilled the law for all who would trust in Him by faith for salvation. The believer needs nothing else to be accepted by God. "And you are complete in Him, who is the head of all principality and power" (Colossians 2:10).

> For what the law could not do because it was weak through the flesh, God sending his own Son in the likeness of sinful flesh and for sin, condemned sin in the flesh: That the righteousness of the law might be fulfilled in us who do not walk after the flesh but after the Spirit. (Romans 8:3-4)

This total and complete acceptance by God is the current experience and position of every believer. Each believer can say with confidence, "I am accepted in the Beloved." This assurance is neither based on who a believer is or is not, nor what a believer does or does not do. Acceptance by God is based solely on the reality that by His grace God has made the believer acceptable to Himself through a spiritual re-creation. This acceptability has been purchased by the precious blood of Christ. The believer's total and complete acceptance by God is through his vital union with Christ.

Chapter 6
An Inheritance

> In whom we have also **obtained an inheritance**,...
> (Ephesians 1:11a, KJBT)

In this verse, the Apostle Paul mentions another spiritual blessing which belongs to the believer. It is the believer's inheritance. Again, Paul points out the source of this blessing. It is obtained by being in Christ. Every one of a believer's spiritual blessings is obtained through his vital union with Christ.

What is this inheritance the believer has obtained? A good explanation of the character of the believer's inheritance is found in the book of I Peter 1:3-5. Peter makes four definitive statements about the believer's inheritance in these verses.

> Blessed be the God and Father of our Lord Jesus Christ, who according to his abundant mercy has begotten us again unto a living hope by the resurrection of Jesus Christ from the dead, *To an inheritance* incorruptible, and undefiled, and that does not fade away, reserved in heaven for you, Who are kept by the power of God through faith unto salvation ready to be revealed in the last time. (I Peter 1:3-5)

First, Peter states this inheritance is "incorruptible" which means there is neither decay nor any possibility of decay in it. This inheritance has not been and cannot be touched by the curse of sin. Every consequence of Adam's sin has been removed from this inheritance. Since the believer's inheritance is incorruptible, it cannot be in this world.

Second, the inheritance is declared to be "undefiled." It is inherently pure and unstained by sin. There is no impurity whatsoever anywhere in it. No sin has, nor ever will stain this inheritance. It is also obtained in an honest manner. There can be neither fraud, nor dishonesty in gaining access to this inheritance. It is a provision of God for His children.

The third quality mentioned about this inheritance is it "does not fade away." The brilliance of the believer's inheritance will never dim. This inheritance will maintain its original brightness forever and ever. Its beauty and perfection will be enjoyed for all eternity by the children of God. All this is a way of saying, "the new will never wear off."

The final words of the explanation are the believer's inheritance "is reserved in heaven for you, who are kept by the power of God through faith." This inheritance could not be on this earth, for it would be defiled and corrupted by the consequences of the curse of sin. It is in Heaven. This inheritance is in God's keeping for the believer's eternal future. The only way to have a place reserved in this marvelous inheritance is to trust in Christ for salvation.

Peter gives additional details concerning the believer's inheritance in the third chapter of II Peter. This earth with the curse and all of the consequences of the curse will be no more. The believer looks forward to the promise of inheriting the new heavens and a new earth in which absolute righteousness will be the order of all things.

> But the day of the Lord will come as a thief in the night; in which the heavens shall pass away with a great noise, and the elements shall melt with fervent heat, the earth also and the works that are in it shall be burned up. Seeing then that all these things shall be dissolved, what manner of persons

> should you be in all holy conduct and godliness, As you are looking for and hasting unto the coming of the day of God, in which the heavens being on fire shall be dissolved, and the elements shall melt with fervent heat? Nevertheless we, according to his promise, look for new heavens and a new earth, in which dwells righteousness. (II Peter 3:10-13)

The Apostle John gives this account of what he saw concerning the believer's promised inheritance. None of the consequences of sin's curse will plague the believer as he enjoys his inheritance forever and ever. This inheritance is a place of absolute perfection provided by the absolutely perfect living God.

> And I saw a new heaven and a new earth: for the first heaven and the first earth had passed away; and there was no more sea. And I John saw the holy city, New Jerusalem, coming down from God out of heaven, prepared as a bride adorned for her husband. And I heard a great voice out of heaven saying, Behold, the tabernacle of God is with men, and he will dwell with them, and they shall be his people, and God himself shall be with them, and be their God. And God shall wipe away all tears from their eyes; and there shall be no more death, neither sorrow, nor crying, neither shall there be any more pain: for the former things have passed away. And he who sat upon the throne said, Behold, I make all things new. And he said unto me, Write: for these words are true and faithful.
> (Revelation 21:1-5)

This inheritance which belongs to every believer is a glorious place. Gold, to which man gives great value on this earth, is just paving material in the city of the believer's inheritance. This city is permeated by the glory of its Builder and Maker.

> And the twelve gates were twelve pearls; every individual gate was of one pearl: and the street of the city was pure gold, like transparent glass. And I saw no temple in it: for the Lord God Almighty and the Lamb are its temple. And the city had no need of the sun, neither of the moon, to shine in it: for the glory of God did light it, and the Lamb is its light. (Revelation 21:21-23)

The believer's inheritance is the city for which Abraham looked as he journeyed throughout the Promised Land. Every believer should be looking excitedly for this city.

> By faith Abraham, when he was called to go out into a place which he would later receive for an inheritance, obeyed; and he went out, not knowing where he was going. By faith he sojourned in the land of promise, as in a strange country, dwelling in tents with Isaac and Jacob, the heirs with him of the same promise: For he looked for a city which has foundations, whose builder and maker is God. (Hebrews 11:8-10)

This is the inheritance Jesus Christ promised to His disciples just before His crucifixion as He was preparing them for His departure. The place Jesus promised is the future eternal dwelling place of all those who put their faith in Him. Any promise is only as sure as the word and character of the one who makes the promise. This promise from Christ is absolutely sure because of who He is.

> Let not your heart be troubled: you believe in God, believe also in me. In my Father's house are many mansions: if it were not so, I would have told you. I go to prepare a place for you. And if I go and prepare a place for you, I will come again, and

> receive you unto myself; that where I am, there you may be also. (John 14:1-3)

This inheritance is an absolute certainty for the believer. Since it is impossible for God to lie, believers can have complete confidence in His promise of an inheritance. "Knowing that from the Lord you shall receive the reward of the inheritance: for you serve the Lord Christ" (Colossians 3:24).

> Thus God, willing more abundantly to show unto the heirs of promise the immutability of his counsel, confirmed it by an oath: That by two immutable things, in which it was impossible for God to lie, we might have a strong consolation, who have fled for refuge to lay hold upon the hope set before us. (Hebrews 6:17-18)

Jesus Himself said one day this earth will pass away. "Heaven and earth shall pass away: but my words shall not pass away" (Luke 21:33). Believers, however, have the promise of an eternal inheritance.

> And for this reason He is the Mediator of the new covenant, that by means of death, for the redemption of the transgressions that were under the first covenant, they who are called might receive the promise of eternal inheritance. (Hebrews 9:15)

This inheritance is a far better possession than anything one may possess on this earth. Jesus asked this question. "For what shall it profit a man, if he shall gain the whole world, and loses his own soul?" (Mark 8:36).

> For you had compassion on me in my chains, and took joyfully the spoiling of your goods, knowing in

yourselves that you have in heaven a better and an enduring possession. (Hebrews 10:34)

Ephesians 1:7a reveals that every believer has "obtained an inheritance." That means that the inheritance is a present possession. By what means may this inheritance be obtained? This verse also gives the means by which it is obtained. It is obtained "in Christ." It can only be obtained through a vital relationship with Christ through faith in His work on the cross.

Christ purchased this inheritance for believers through the shedding of His blood on the cross. He gives it to every person who trusts Him by faith for salvation. It cannot be purchased. It can neither be earned by good works, nor acquired through self-effort. It can only be obtained by faith.

Believers are made fit or qualified for this inheritance by being delivered from the power of darkness. "Giving thanks unto the Father, who has made us fit to be partakers of the inheritance of the saints in light: Who has delivered us from the power of darkness, and has translated us into the kingdom of his dear Son" (Colossians 1:12-13).

Those who are in Christ are made fit or qualified for this inheritance by having been made new in Christ. "Therefore, if any man is in Christ, he is a new creation: old things have passed away; behold, all things have become new" (II Corinthians 5:17). No human could ever reform himself to the point he could fit into this inheritance because perfect righteousness and complete holiness are the required qualifications. The only perfect righteousness and complete holiness a human can possess is the righteousness and holiness of Christ. Christ's righteousness and holiness are given to all those who put their faith in Him.

Through faith in Christ, believers are the children of God. As His children they are heirs as well. Believers are joint heirs with

Christ who is heir of all things. Believers are heirs to everything to which Christ is heir. Believers are heirs to everything which is included in the new heavens and the new earth. This glorious inheritance is a gift from God's superabounding grace to everyone who is in Christ by faith.

> God, who at various times and in different ways spoke unto the fathers in times past by the prophets, Has in these last days spoken unto us by his Son, whom he has appointed heir of all things, by whom also he made the worlds (Hebrews 1:1-2)
>
> The Spirit himself bears witness with our spirit that we are the children of God: And if children then heirs; heirs of God, and joint heirs with Christ; for if we suffer with him we will also be glorified together. (Romans 8:16-17)
>
> And because you are sons, God has sent forth the Spirit of his Son into your hearts, crying, Abba, Father. Therefore, you are no longer a servant, but a son; and if a son, then an heir of God through Christ. (Galatians 4:6-7)
>
> That being justified by his grace, we should be made heirs according to the hope of eternal life." (Titus 3:7)

Believers in all ages have looked forward to the inheritance which God has promised to those who trust in Him. Those who are in Christ today look for the same inheritance for which the saints of old looked.

> These all died in faith, not having received the promises, but having seen them far off, and were persuaded of them, and embraced them, and

confessed that they were strangers and pilgrims on the earth. For they who say such things declare plainly that they seek a country. And truly, if they had been mindful of that country from where they came out, they might have had opportunity to have returned. But now they desire a better country, that is, a heavenly: therefore God is not ashamed to be called their God: for he has prepared a city for them. (Hebrews 11:13-16)

There is coming a future day "in which the heavens shall pass away with a great noise, and the elements shall melt with fervent heat, the earth also and the works that are in it shall be burned up" (II Peter 3:10b). When the day comes and all creation ceases to be, God will still be, and believers will still be. In God's presence, believers will enjoy their eternal inheritance which He has prepared for them. This eternal inheritance has been given to everyone who is in Christ.

Chapter 7
Sealed with the Holy Spirit

> That we who first trusted in Christ should be to the praise of his glory. In whom you also trusted, after you heard the word of truth, the gospel of your salvation: in whom also after you believed, you were **sealed with the Holy Spirit** of promise, Who is the down payment on our inheritance until the redemption of the purchased possession, unto the praise of his glory. (Ephesians 1:12-14, KJBT)

The believer has been sealed with the Holy Spirit. However, there are two important words in this passage which preclude the spiritual blessing of being sealed with the Holy Spirit. Those two words are "heard" and "believed." The Ephesians had "heard the word of truth, the gospel of your salvation," and had "believed" in Christ for their own salvation. When they believed in Christ, they were sealed with the Holy Spirit.

> For whoever shall call upon the name of the Lord shall be saved. How then shall they call on him in whom they have not believed? And how shall they believe in him of whom they have not heard? And how shall they hear without a preacher?
> (Romans 10:13-14)

Being "sealed with the Holy Spirit" is not something which happens subsequent to salvation. It is an integral part of the salvation experience. One receives the Holy Spirit at the time of salvation. It is the Holy Spirit who brings the believer to life spiritually. "It is the Spirit who gives life; the flesh profits nothing" (John 6:33a).

> But after that the kindness and love of God our Savior toward man appeared, Not by works of righteousness which we have done, but according to his mercy he saved us, by the washing of regeneration, and renewing of the Holy Spirit; Which he shed on us abundantly through Jesus Christ our Savior. (Titus 3:4-6)

At the moment one is regenerated by the Holy Spirit, the Holy Spirit indwells the believer. He comes into and lives within all who place their faith in Christ for salvation. The presence of the Holy Spirit in the believer validates the reality of his salvation. "By this we know that we dwell in him, and he in us, because he has given us of his Spirit" (I John 4:13).

One must understand the meaning of the word sealed in this verse to understand how special this spiritual blessing is. The metaphor of the Holy Spirit being a seal comes from the common practice of applying an official stamp, insignia, signature or some other identifying mark to a document to verify it is an official document. A notary seal one would get to show a document is valid or official is a similar type seal one would recognize today. Another example is from ancient times. An official document from a king would be sealed with hot wax. The king would then press his insignia ring into the soft wax and leave its imprint to verify it was an official document from the king.

Official seals were and are used especially on legal documents. A seal or stamp is used to show a finished transaction. Sometimes a seal is needed to verify ownership. Often a seal is needed to establish the authenticity of an item. There are times when a seal is required to confirm a person's authority. The purpose of requiring a seal on a document is to show the document is genuine and to guarantee it is neither fake, nor forged. This illustration concerning a seal or stamp paints a wonderful picture of the Holy Spirit in the life of every believer.

The death of Christ on the cross completed the transaction once and for all who would believe on Him. "For Christ also has suffered once for sins, the just for the unjust, that he might bring us to God, being put to death in the flesh, but made alive by the Spirit" (I Peter 3:18).

> For Christ has not entered into the holy places made with hands, which are the copies of the true; but into heaven itself, now to appear in the presence of God for us: Nor yet that he should offer himself often, as the high priest enters into the holy place every year with blood of others; For then he must have suffered often since the foundation of the world: but now once in the end of the ages he has appeared to put away sin by the sacrifice of himself. (Hebrews 9:24-26)

A transaction usually requires some sort of seal to show the transaction has been satisfactorily completed. The seal or indwelling presence of the Holy Spirit assures the believer the satisfactory payment for his sin debt has been paid by the death and resurrection of the Christ. God's holiness, justice and righteousness are satisfied with Christ's sacrifice of Himself to put away sin. For those who put their faith in Christ, the Holy Spirit is the authenticating seal showing the transaction has been completed. "Now we have not received the spirit of the world, but the Spirit who is from God; that we might know the things that are freely given to us by God" (I Corinthians 2:12).

A seal is also used on documents to verify ownership of an item or a property. The seal or presence of the Holy Spirit in the life of a believer verifies he belongs to God. Those who are in Christ by faith are the people of God. They have been purchased by God. They belong to Him. They are His own special people. Those who were previously nothing are now the people of God through faith. The Holy Spirit is the seal verifying God's ownership of each one who by faith is in a vital union with Christ.

> What? Do you not know that your body is the temple of the Holy Spirit who is in you, whom you have of God, and you are not your own? For you are bought with a price: therefore glorify God in your body, and in your spirit, which are God's.
> (I Corinthians 6:19-20)

> But you are a chosen race, a royal priesthood, a holy nation, his own special people; that you should show forth the praises of him who has called you out of darkness into his marvelous light: Who in time past were not a people, but are now the people of God: who had not obtained mercy, but now have obtained mercy. (I Peter 2:9-10)

When one is purchasing a collectible item, some type of seal of authenticity is usually required. An example would be a limited-edition art print. It will be both numbered and signed by the artist and will come with a statement of authenticity. The Holy Spirit is the authenticating seal letting the believer know he is an authentic child of God. "The Spirit himself bears witness with our spirit that we are the children of God" (Romans 8:16).

It is only by the presence of the Holy Spirit in their lives believers are able to recognize God as their Heavenly Father. The complete change of thinking toward God the Holy Spirit produces authenticates the believer's new position in Christ. The seal or indwelling presence of the Holy Spirit assures the believer he is a child of God.

> So then they who are in the flesh cannot please God.
> But you are not in the flesh but in the Spirit, if the

> Spirit of God dwells in you. Now if any man does not have the Spirit of Christ he is not His.
> (Romans 8:7-8)

When a person represents someone else, he needs a means to confirm he possesses the authority to represent the person. Believers are authorized to be witnesses to who Christ is and to what He provides. The Holy Spirit is the seal which authorizes the believer as a representative of Christ in this world.

> But you shall receive power, after that the Holy Spirit has come upon you: and you shall be witnesses unto me both in Jerusalem, and in all Judea, and in Samaria, and unto the uttermost part of the earth. (Acts 1:8)

In Ephesians 1:14 the Holy Spirit is also said to be the "down payment" on the believer's inheritance. The believer's inheritance was discussed in the previous chapter. A down payment is the guarantee of the intention to complete a transaction. The down payment is also a portion of the total payment. The indwelling of the Holy Spirit could thus be said to be a little bit of Heaven God has given to each believer while he lives in this world. This down payment is the guarantee of the believer's complete redemption with an eternity in Heaven. The soul of a believer is currently redeemed, but he looks forward the redemption of the body as well. Ephesians 1:14 states that this down payment is "until the redemption of the purchased possession" at which time the believer is glorified. The believer will go from growing in the Lord to being with the Lord.

There are a couple of things about the Holy Spirit in these verses which need to be pointed out as well. First, it is important to remember "Holy" is not the first name of the Spirit of God. It is a statement of His character. His character is holy because He is

God. Since the Holy Spirit is God, His presence in the believer makes the believer a partaker of the divine nature.

> According as his divine power has given unto us all things that pertain unto life and godliness, through the knowledge of him who has called us to glory and virtue: By which are given unto us exceedingly great and precious promises: that by these you might be partakers of the divine nature, having escaped the corruption that is in the world through lust. (II Peter 1:3-4)

Second, He is said to be the "Holy Spirit of promise." When Jesus was preparing His disciples for His departure, He promised them another Comforter. The Holy Spirit is the Comforter. Jesus promised Him to His followers.

> And I will pray the Father, and he shall give you another Comforter, that he may abide with you forever; Even the Spirit of truth; whom the world cannot receive, because it does not see him, neither knows him: but you know him; for he dwells with you, and shall be in you. (John 14:16-17)

> But when the Comforter has come, whom I will send unto you from the Father, even the Spirit of truth, who proceeds from the Father, he shall testify of me. (John 15:26)

In summary, the seal of the Holy Spirit is the guarantee the transaction for the payment of the believer's sin debt has been completed. He is the seal who verifies believers are God's own special people. The indwelling presence of the Holy Spirit authenticates the believer's position as a child of God and also authorizes him to be a representative of Christ in this world.

The Holy Spirit is also the down payment guaranteeing God's intention to fulfill His promise of an eternal inheritance to those who are in Christ.

It is worth noting the phrase "the praise of His glory" occurs twice in Ephesians 1:12-14. When a phrase appears twice this close together, it usually means the writer wanted to emphasize it. God saves to "the praise of His glory." God gives the Holy Spirit unto "the praise of His glory."

All God does for a believer is for the purpose of bringing glorious praise to Himself. All spiritual blessings He gives to believers are to bring glorious praise to Himself as well.

Galatians 5:16-26

16 This I say then, Walk in the Spirit, and you shall not fulfill the lust of the flesh.

17 For the flesh lusts against the Spirit, and the Spirit against the flesh: and these are contrary the one to the other: so that you cannot do the things that you would.

18 But if you are led by the Spirit, you are not under the law.

19 Now the works of the flesh are manifest, which are these; adultery, sexual immorality, uncleanness, lewdness,

20 Idolatry, witchcraft, hatred, disputes, jealousy, wrath, strife, seditions, heresies,

21 Envy, murders, drunkenness, revelry, and such like: concerning which I tell you beforehand, as I have also told you in time past, that they who do such things shall not inherit the kingdom of God.

22 But the fruit of the Spirit is love, joy, peace, longsuffering, gentleness, goodness, faith,

23 Meekness, temperance: against such there is no law.

24 And they who are Christ's have crucified the flesh with its affections and lusts.

25 If we live in the Spirit, let us also walk in the Spirit.

26 Let us not become conceited, provoking one another, envying one another. (KJBT)

Chapter 8
Enlightened

Therefore I also, after I heard of your faith in the Lord Jesus, and love unto all the saints, Do not cease to give thanks for you, making mention of you in my prayers; That the God of our Lord Jesus Christ, the Father of glory, may give unto you the spirit of wisdom and revelation in the knowledge of him: The eyes of your **understanding being enlightened**; that you may know what the hope of his calling is, and what the riches of the glory of his inheritance in the saints.
(Ephesians 1:15-18, KJBT)

These verses are the first half of an extensive prayer the Apostle Paul constantly prays for the Ephesian believers. In the middle of this portion of Scripture is another of the spiritual blessings which belongs to a believer because of his vital union with Christ. The blessing is found in the phrase, "The eyes of your understanding being enlightened" (Ephesians 1:18a).

Before coming to faith in Christ, the spiritual eyes of believers were blinded by the god of this world. The phrase "understanding being enlightened" is a statement of the fact something happened to them when they had repented and trusted in Christ. A clear way of stating the idea of "being enlightened" would be to use the phrase, "having been enlightened." "Having been enlightened" makes it clear enlightenment is something which occurred at salvation and was currently in effect in them. The "eyes of your understanding" is referring to the spiritual eyes of believers. This spiritual enlightenment was a necessary prerequisite for Paul's prayers for them to be answered.

> But if our gospel is hidden, it is hidden to those who are lost: In whom the god of this world has blinded the minds of those who do not believe, lest the light of the glorious gospel of Christ, who is the image of God, should shine unto them. For we do not preach ourselves, but Christ Jesus the Lord; and ourselves your servants for Jesus' sake. For God, who commanded the light to shine out of darkness, has shined in our hearts, to give the light of the knowledge of the glory of God in the face of Jesus Christ. (II Corinthians 4:3-6)

What does enlightened mean? The simplest definition is to shed light on something. A synonym which comes to mind is the word illuminate. The basic idea is to dispel darkness by providing light so one can see something clearly. The brighter the light, the more clearly one can see. Through the enlightenment they had received in Christ, they had been given a new capacity for understanding spiritual matters. This new capacity comes to a believer as the result of his heart and mind being illuminated through his acceptance of the glorious gospel of Christ.

Believers have been given a present and continuing spiritual enlightenment. Because of this, they are able to see clearly the things that last forever. Before their redemption, all unbelievers were not only in darkness, but also were the very source of darkness. "For once you were darkness, but now you are light in the Lord: walk as children of light:" (Ephesians 5:8). Every person starts out in life with his spiritual understanding darkened.

> This I say therefore, and testify in the Lord, that from now on you do not walk as other Gentiles walk, in the futility of their mind, Having the understanding darkened, being alienated from the life of God through the ignorance that is in them,

because of the blindness of their heart: (Ephesians 4:17-18)

The believer was called out of this darkness. Christ "has called you out of darkness into his marvelous light" (I Peter 2:10b). Having been enlightened means a person who had been in spiritual darkness and could neither understand nor discern spiritual realities is now able to clearly comprehend those eternal realities. Now that they have been enlightened, Paul prays for several things they might understand with their new capacity to comprehend spiritual truths.

Paul prays the believers would be given the spirit of wisdom and of revelation. He is not asking for them to be given the Holy Spirit. He had just previously said they had been "sealed with the Holy Spirit of promise." He is not talking about the human spirit, because the human spirit is spiritually dead and cannot understand spiritual things. "But the natural man does not receive the things of the Spirit of God, for they are foolishness to him; nor can he know them, because they are spiritually discerned." (I Corinthians 2:14).

When Paul writes "spirit of wisdom," he is referring to the regenerated spirit of the believer. The spirit of man which had been dead and alienated from God has now been brought to life and enlightened by the Holy Spirit. Through his newly enlivened and enlightened spirit, a believer has this new capacity to understand spiritual truth and look into the deep things of God.

> But as it is written, Eye has not seen, nor ear heard, neither has entered into the heart of man, the things which God has prepared for those who love him. But God has revealed them unto us by his Spirit: for the Spirit searches all things, yes, the deep things of God. For what man knows the things of a man except the spirit of man which is in him?

> Even so the things of God no man knows, except the Spirit of God. Now we have not received the spirit of the world, but the Spirit who is from God; that we might know the things that are freely given to us by God. Which things we also do not speak in the words which man's wisdom teaches, but which the Holy Spirit teaches; comparing spiritual things with spiritual. (I Corinthians 2:9-13)

Paul prays that through the believer's new spiritual capacity, he will also have a spirit of revelation. His prayer is each believer will have a comprehensive insight into what has been revealed by God. His desire is as they read and study the Word of God, they will clearly comprehend and understand the eternal realities revealed in it.

Spiritual wisdom and insight come to the believer "in the knowledge of Him" (Ephesians 1:17b). It comes through a full and thorough knowledge of Christ. This must be an experiential and personal knowledge of Christ Himself. It is not just an intellectual knowledge about Christ. The more acquainted with Christ a believer becomes, the more spiritual wisdom he gains, and the clearer his insight will be into those things which have been revealed by God.

Generally defined, wisdom is knowing how to apply truth to life. The meaning of wisdom in this passage then is knowing how to apply the newly enlightened spiritual understandings to one's new life in Christ. Paul's prayer for them is this new ability to apply revealed truth to their daily lives would be their new reality.

When Paul prays for the spirit of wisdom and revelation, he is praying that through their spiritual blessing of enlightenment they will be able to comprehend those things which are hidden from the natural mind. Those things which they could not comprehend before because of their spiritual blindness would now be in full view. Spiritual mysteries which were hidden from the natural mind are revealed to the spiritual mind through the glorious gospel of Christ.

> But if our gospel is hidden, it is hidden to those who are lost: In whom the god of this world has blinded the minds of those who do not believe, lest the light of the glorious gospel of Christ, who is the image of God, should shine unto them. (II Corinthians 4:3-4)

The spirit of wisdom and the spirit of revelation are given to believers by their Heavenly Father, so they will be able to understand biblical principles revealed in the Scriptures and apply those principles to every situation they face in life. Having been enlightened, a believer is now able obey the command to "be renewed in the spirit" of his mind (Ephesians 4:23).

Paul shares two other prayer requests in this section. They follow the statement believers have been enlightened. The requests are, "that you may know what the hope of His calling is, and what the riches of the glory of His inheritance in the saints" (Ephesians 1:18b). Since they have been enlightened, they now have the capacity to know and to understand these spiritual realities.

Believers now have the spiritual ability to know what the hope of His calling is. Paul prays they will fully comprehend this calling. This hope is neither a wish, nor a dream. The believer's hope is the reality of an assured expectation of eternal salvation. Believers have this hope because it is the hope to which "the God of our Lord Jesus Christ, the Father of glory," has called them. Paul is not referring to the location of the believer's hope, but rather the attitude of looking forward to his assured expectation. The believer's looking forward to deliverance with this assured expectation sustains and encourages him in the toughest of times.

> But remember the former days, in which, after you were illuminated, you endured a great struggle with afflictions; Partly, while you were made a gazing stock both by reproaches and afflictions; and partly, while you became companions of those who were so treated. For you had compassion on me in my chains, and took joyfully the spoiling of your goods, knowing in yourselves that you have in heaven a better and an enduring possession. Therefore do not throw away your confidence, which has great compensation of reward. For you need to have patience, that, after you have done the will of God, you might receive the promise. (Hebrews 10:32-36)

Paul's final prayer for them in this portion of Scripture is for the believers to know and to understand their value to God. Believers are God's own particular, special, precious, chosen possession. Believers are His wealth. He paid a great price for them. The price is the precious blood of His only begotten Son Jesus Christ. The magnitude of the price shows every believer his personal value to God.

Believers are God's glorious inheritance (Ephesians 1:18c). He is glorified in believers by the demonstration of His grace in saving sinners and making them fit for Heaven. Believers are more valuable to God than all of the rest of His glorious creation. When the heavens have passed away, when the elements have melted with fervent heat, and when the earth with all its works have been burned up, believers will still be and will be dwelling with their Heavenly Father.

Chapter 9
Empowered

> And what the **exceeding greatness of his power** toward us who believe is, according to the working of his mighty power, Which he worked in Christ, when he raised him from the dead, and set him at his own right hand in the heavenly places, Far above all principality, and power, and might, and dominion, and every name that is named, not only in this world, but also in that which is to come: And has put all things under his feet, and made him the head over all things to the church.
> (Ephesians 1:19-22, KJBT)

Ephesians 1:19-22 is the second part of Paul's prayer he began in Ephesians 1:17. The first part of the prayer was discussed in the previous chapter concerning the spiritual blessing of enlightenment. All Paul's requests in the prayer are based on a new reality. The spiritual eyes of believers have been enlightened and now they can comprehend spiritual truths. His prayer for them is since they have been enlightened, they will have a clear understanding and appreciation of the power now at work in them. He is not praying they would receive power because God's power is already in every believer through the indwelling presence of the Holy Spirit. The power of God at work in the life of a believer is a spiritual blessing every believer needs to understand more fully.

God's power is sufficient to save every person who will trust Him for salvation. "For I am not ashamed of the gospel of Christ: for it is the power of God unto salvation to everyone who believes; to the Jew first and also to the Greek" (Romans 1:16). God's power is not only sufficient to save the believer, but also sufficient to empower the believer for living every day in Christ. "According as His divine power has given unto us all things that pertain unto life and godliness" (II Peter 2:3a). Paul's desire for the Ephesian believers is that they might have a greater knowledge and understanding of the "exceeding greatness of His power" (Ephesians 1:19).

In Ephesians 3:20 Paul also declares God's power is at work in the life of believers, "Now unto him who is able to do exceedingly abundantly above all that we ask or think, according to the power that works in us." God's power is beyond inexhaustible. His power is more than enough power to accomplish what needs to be done in any situation. God's power is limitless. Through the superabundance of His power, He is able to answer the prayers of believers and to do far more than believers can even imagine.

God's power is incomparable and inexhaustible. His power far surpasses any need a believer could ever have. It is far more than enough to confront any consequence of the curse of sin a believer may face in this world. The "exceeding greatness of His power" is also proclaimed in the book of Hebrews.

> God, who at various times and in different ways spoke unto the fathers in times past by the prophets, Has in these last days spoken unto us by his Son, whom he has appointed heir of all things, by whom also he made the worlds; Who being the brightness of his glory, and the express image of his person, and upholding all things by the word of his power, when he had by himself purged our sins, sat down on the right hand of the Majesty on high. (Hebrews 1:1-3)

This exceedingly great power of God is "toward us who believe." This means God's superabundant power is working on behalf of every believer. Not only has His great power worked in saving believers, but His great power is also at work on behalf of believers and within believers. His power is available and sufficient for whatever a believer might face in his daily life.

The Apostle Paul wants to make sure believers become aware of how awesome God's power really is. In the opening phrase of Ephesians 1:19-20 there are four references to power in the text. According to Kenneth Wuest, Paul uses four different Greek words for those four references. "And what the exceeding greatness of his *power (dunamis)* toward us who believe is, according to the *working (energia)* of his *mighty(kratos) power(ischus)*" (Ephesians 1:19). These four words give an overview of God's exceedingly great power *(Wuest's Word Studies from the Greek New Testament, (1940-1955).*

Dunamis is the word from which the English word dynamite comes. Dunamis is about the dynamic power of the all-powerful Living God. It is the powerful capability to act which God has within Himself.

Energia is the word from which the English word energy originates. Energia means strength at work. God is exercising His power when He saves lost souls. God's power operates in a believer which enables him to follow Christ. God's power is the energizing force in the believer's life.

Kratos is the forceful manifestation of strength. Kratos means the power to rule or master. The power to rule indicates it is power which overcomes all resistance or opposition.

Ischus has the idea of inherent power. God has more power in Himself than He could ever need.

God's dynamic explosive power as expressed in these four words is fully operational on behalf of every believer. God's exceedingly great power will manifest itself by giving the believer victory in every life situation he faces. God's awesome, immeasurable power is at work in every believer.

The Apostle Paul uses four illustrations to demonstrate the exceeding greatness of God's power which is at work in and for the believer. These examples of God's power are found in Ephesians 1:20-23.

First, he points out this mighty power is the power "Which He worked in Christ, when He raised him from the dead" (Ephesians 1:20a). This very same operative power was at work in raising Christ from the dead is the operative power in saving every person who is redeemed. This resurrection power not only saves, but also continues to be operative in the daily life of every believer.

Next, Paul reveals the power of the heavenly throne. "And set him at his own right hand in the heavenly places" (Ephesians 1:20b). From the position of honor and authority at His Father's right hand, Christ exercises dominion over the physical universe. From this position of authority and power He rules all creation. Jesus Christ summarized it with these words, "All power is given unto me in heaven and in earth" (Matthew 28:18b).

The third illustration of Christ's power is the statement of His supremacy over all spiritual beings and every earthly power (Ephesians 1:21-22a). Christ's power is far above all spiritual beings. Christ is over and leader of the heavenly hosts as the "Captain of the Lord's hosts" (Joshua 5:15). Through the shedding of His blood on the cross, Christ has dominion over the evil hosts (Colossians 2:14-15). Christ also has dominion over every government or authority which exists on this earth. The dominion of Christ over all powers either in the spiritual world or on this earth is absolute, for they have been put under His feet. His power is far greater than all other powers combined.

Since Christ's power is far above any spiritual power, the believer has the power to overcome his evil adversary. "You are of God, little children, and have overcome them: because greater is He who is in you, than he who is in the world" (I John 4:4). Victory over all the forces of hell has been won by the by the death and resurrection of Christ. The power of His victory belongs to every believer.

The final illustration of the power of Christ Paul gives is Christ's position in the Church. "And made him the head over all things to the church, which is his body, the fullness of him who fills all in all" (Ephesians 1:22b-23). The Church is not an organization, but rather a living organism composed of all who trust Christ as Savior. Any living organism must have a head with the power of decision and control for the total organism. God has made Christ the Head of the Church. Not only is He the Head of the Church, but He also is the One Who fills every believer with His presence by the Holy Spirit.

The exceedingly great power of God works on behalf of the believer in saving him. "For the preaching of the cross is to those who perish foolishness; but unto us who are saved it is the power of God" (I Corinthians 1:18). It is this same dynamic, inexhaustible power which also works in the believer to re-make him into the image of Christ. "For whom he did foreknow, he also did predestinate to be conformed to the image of his Son" (Romans 8:29a). The Apostle Peter also points out a believer's life is changed by the divine power at work in his life.

> Simon Peter, a servant and an apostle of Jesus Christ, to those who have obtained like precious faith with us through the righteousness of God and our Savior Jesus Christ: Grace and peace be

multiplied unto you through the knowledge of God, and of Jesus our Lord, According as his divine power has given unto us all things that pertain unto life and godliness, through the knowledge of him who has called us to glory and virtue: By which are given unto us exceedingly great and precious promises: that by these you might be partakers of the divine nature, having escaped the corruption that is in the world through lust. And besides this, giving all diligence, add to your faith virtue; and to virtue knowledge; And to knowledge self-control; and to self-control patience; and to patience godliness; And to godliness brotherly kindness; and to brotherly kindness love. For if these things are in you, and abound, they make you that you shall neither be barren nor unfruitful in the knowledge of our Lord Jesus Christ. (II Peter 1:1-8)

*This mighty power of God is at work **for** every believer, and it is at work **in** every believer.* The Apostle Paul prays for those who are in a vital union with Christ through faith to comprehend and to fully experience the exceedingly great power which has been given to them by their Heavenly Father.

God's limitless and inexhaustible power is at work in every believer. The only thing which can limit God's power in the life of a believer is the believer's lack of faith.

Chapter 10
Made Spiritually Alive

And He has **made you alive**, who were dead in trespasses and sins; In time past you walked according to the course of this world, according to the prince of the power of the air, the spirit that now works in the children of disobedience: Among whom we also all had our way of living in times past in the lusts of our flesh, fulfilling the desires of the flesh and of the mind; and were by nature the children of wrath, even as others. But God, who is rich in mercy, for His great love with which He loved us, Even when we were dead in sins, has made us alive together with Christ, (by grace you are saved;). (Ephesians 2:1-5, KJBT)

The Apostle Paul's declaration that the Ephesian believers have been "made alive" reveals the next spiritual blessing. They are now alive spiritually. When he states they have been "made alive," he at the same time declares they previously had been spiritually dead. They had been raised from spiritual death to spiritual life.

The Apostle Paul declares their condition before having been made alive. They "were dead in trespasses and sins" (Ephesians 2:1b). This is a clear and unambiguous declaration they had been spiritually dead before salvation. The definition of physical death is a cessation of vital functions or lack of life. When this definition is applied to spiritual death, it means when Adam sinned all of the vital functions of man's spiritual relationship with God ceased, and thus Adam lost his spiritual life.

Humans because of their sin are alienated from the life which is in God. Thus, there is a total lack of spiritual life in any human "Having the understanding darkened, being alienated from the life of God through the ignorance that is in them, because of the blindness of their heart" (Ephesians 4:18). All humans are spiritually dead and in need of spiritual resurrection. "Therefore, as by one man sin entered into the world and death by sin; and so death passed upon all men for all have sinned" (Romans 5:12). "For as in Adam all die" (I Corinthians 15:22a). As someone has said, "Every human is spiritually still-born."

Paul proceeds to explain the characteristics of the spiritually dead condition. In his expansion and elaboration concerning spiritual death, Paul clearly revealed the Ephesians had been totally dead spiritually before salvation.

The Apostle points out that having been spiritually dead, the Ephesians had "walked according to the course of this world" (Ephesians 2:2a). One could paraphrase this to read, the Ephesians had lived according to the spirit of the age. Unbelievers order and direct their lives by the spirit of the age in which they live. Since Adam's sin and fall, humans have been in rebellion against God as well as being in opposition to His plan of the ages. Throughout history, rebellion and opposition have taken different forms depending on the spirit of the particular age. The humanistic philosophies, opinions, thoughts, morals, directives, etc. of the world have controlled unbelievers' thought processes in different ways throughout history. Thinking and living according to spirit of the age determines the way unbelievers live in rebellion and opposition to God.

Paul then reveals who is in control of the spirit of the age. Unbelievers are controlled by the spirit of the age and live their lives "according to the prince of the power of the air, the spirit that now works in the children of disobedience" (Ephesians 2:2b). Satan, the prince of the power of the air, dominates the thinking of the age and thus determines how unbelievers live in rebellion against and in opposition to God. The word power indicates authority. This implies not only Satan, but also his emissaries, the demons, are at work under Satan's authority. The spirit at work in the "children of disobedience" is the spirit of the age which is controlled by the prince of the power of the air who is the enemy of God and the leader of the rebellion against God.

Paul continues showing the unbelievers' way of living before being made alive were dominated by spiritual death. As unbelievers, they had lived like all other unbelievers, "according to the lust of our flesh, fulfilling the desires of the flesh and of the mind" (Ephesians 2:3a). Flesh refers to the human sin nature alienated from God. The sin nature, devoid of life, had full and complete control of the way in which they had lived as unbelievers. Fulfilling the desires of the sin nature and obtaining those things which satisfy the sin nature were the thoughts which dominated their thinking as unbelievers. The only purpose in life was for this world and the satisfaction of desires corrupted by sin. The spirit in rebellion against God and in opposition to God had full sway in their lives before they were made spiritually alive.

Those who have been made alive in Christ were at one time like all others, spiritually dead and under the wrath of God. "Were" is the assertion of a condition which previously existed in the lives of those who have been made alive. It was a continuous and constant condition in which they had been living. Because of their previous nature in trespasses and sins, they had lived as the children of wrath. They had lived every moment of every day with the wrath of God hanging over their heads. God's wrath is on unbelievers because they are condemned. "He who believes on Him is not condemned: but he who does not believe is condemned already because he has not believed in the name of the only begotten Son of God" (John 3:18). "For the wrath of God is revealed from heaven against all ungodliness and unrighteousness of men who hold the truth in unrighteousness"

(Romans 1:18). Faith in Christ is the only way to escape the wrath of God. "He who believes on the Son has everlasting life, and he who does not believe the Son shall not see life but the wrath of God abides on him" (John 3:36).

The turning point for the spiritually dead is the phrase "but God" (Ephesians 2:4a). The only hope for the spiritually dead is the intervention of the living God Himself. Since all humans are born spiritually dead, they cannot help themselves. Dead people are incapable of doing anything to help themselves. God has intervened for those who put their faith in Christ. He raises them from spiritual death and gives them spiritual life in Christ. All life comes from life. Spiritual life must come from spiritual life. Spiritual life can only come from the living God.

Thankfully, God is "rich in mercy" (Ephesians 2:4a). Because of sin, humans are guilty and deserve punishment under the wrath of God. Mercy means withholding the punishment which is due. It is a good thing for humans that God possesses an immeasurable, inexhaustible wealth of mercy by which He withholds the judgment. God's justice demands punishment for sin, but His abundant mercy withholds the punishment. "O give thanks unto the LORD; for he is good: for his mercy endures forever" (Psalm 136:1). The phrase "for his mercy endures forever" is used twenty-six times in Psalm 136.

"His great love with which he loved us" is what moves Him to show mercy to the human race (Ephesians 2:4b). This great love moves God to seek the greatest benefit of the one loved. "For God so loved the world that he gave his only begotten Son that whoever believes in him should not perish but have everlasting life" (John 3:16). This verse shows how far God's love will go to seek the greatest benefit of those He loves. The Apostle John also gives us another declaration of the love of God for those who were created in His image.

> In this was manifested the love of God toward us, because God sent his only begotten Son into the world, that we might live through him. In this is love, not that we loved God, but that he loved us, and sent his Son to be the atoning sacrifice for our sins. (I John 4:9-10)

The final action involved in bringing the spiritually dead to life in Christ is the grace of God. Grace is the undeserved, unearned favor of God shown to those who are in rebellion against Him. The Apostle Paul inserts the parenthetic clause, "(by grace you are saved)" (Ephesians 2:5b), to make it clear this vital union with Christ is given to the believer by the grace of God through the believer's faith in Christ. "For by grace are you saved through faith; and that not of yourselves: it is the gift of God: Not of works, lest any man should boast" (Ephesians 2:8-9).

A believer's change from having been spiritually dead to being made spiritually alive comes as the result of his faith connection with Christ. "And you, being dead in your sins and the uncircumcision of your flesh, has he made alive together with him, having forgiven you all trespasses" (Colossians 2:13).

The Apostle Peter addresses the new life of a believer in an interesting way. "You also, as living stones, are built up a spiritual house, a holy priesthood, to offer up spiritual sacrifices, acceptable to God by Jesus Christ" (I Peter 2:4). Unbelievers are as spiritually dead as a rock. It is obvious a rock has neither life, nor potential for life in itself. Neither does a human have spiritual life, nor the potential for spiritual life in himself. Peter points out those who were stone cold dead spiritually are now alive spiritually as "living stones." Those who were spiritually dead as a rock can only be made alive through faith in Jesus Christ.

The Apostle Paul also gives this explanation of what it means to be made alive in Christ. The spiritual life the believer now possesses comes from the fact Christ is living in the believer through the indwelling presence of the Holy Spirit.

> For I through the law am dead to the law, that I might live unto God. I am crucified with Christ: nevertheless I live; yet not I, but Christ lives in me: and the life which I now live in the flesh I live by faith in the Son of God, who loved me, and gave himself for me. (Galatians 2:19-20)

There is a drastic change of thinking between the spiritually dead person a believer once was and spiritually alive person he now is. The new thinking pattern for the believer is controlled by the Holy Spirit. This new thinking produces a focus on the things which last forever in one who is now spiritually alive.

> For what the law could not do because it was weak through the flesh, God sending his own Son in the likeness of sinful flesh and for sin, condemned sin in the flesh: That the righteousness of the law might be fulfilled in us who do not walk after the flesh but after the Spirit. For they who live according to the flesh do mind the things of the flesh; but they who live according to the Spirit the things of the Spirit. For to be carnally minded is death but to be spiritually minded is life and peace.
> (Romans 8:3-6)

Chapter 11
God's Workmanship

> For by grace are you saved through faith; and that not of yourselves: it is the gift of God: Not of works, lest any man should boast. For **we are his workmanship**, created in Christ Jesus unto good works, which God has before ordained that we should walk in them. (Ephesians 2:8-10, KJBT)

The Apostle Paul makes a wonderful declaration in these verses when he writes "we are His workmanship." It is a truly spiritual blessing to be the spiritual workmanship of the glorious Designer, the Creator.

What does the word workmanship mean? Literally it means something which is made. It could be stated as one's handiwork. Workmanship could be a piece of art painted by an artist. It could be a beautiful piece of furniture designed and built by a craftsman. Workmanship is the handiwork of a skilled designer and builder in any field.

God is the Designer of everything that is. He who created all things and holds them all together by the word of His power is the One who designed and provides the believer's salvation. This salvation which He designed is perfect in every way. God created everything including humans with absolute perfection in the beginning. Creation's perfection was destroyed by man's fall into sin. In Christ, the believer's perfect spiritual standing before God has been created anew. Every believer's salvation is the workmanship of the living God.

A piece of canvas could never cover itself with a beautiful work of art. A stack of wood could never form itself into a beautiful piece of furniture; so neither can a sinner cover himself with a glorious salvation. In salvation, God does not improve an old nature; rather He creates a new nature. God by His grace makes the believer a new person. This new spiritual creation is the workmanship of God. "Therefore if any man is in Christ, he is a new creation: old things have passed away; behold, all things have become new" (II Corinthians 5:17).

This salvation which God designed and provided is absolutely perfect. It cannot be improved upon by anything which man can add. There are no works whatsoever involved in one's salvation. Salvation is through faith in Christ alone. Since salvation is the handiwork of God, no human can ever boast about any part he had in his own salvation.

It has often been said God's design for salvation is so perfectly simple nothing can be taken away from it. The only way God's perfect design for salvation can be corrupted is by adding something to it as being necessary for salvation. Throughout the history of the church, man has corrupted God's perfect design by adding various requirements as being necessary for salvation.

A workman begins with a purpose for what he plans to produce. In the believer, God has created a new person with the capacity for producing good works. God has ordained producing good works to be the normal way of living as His new creation. Good works are to be characteristic of those who are in Christ. "Even so, faith, if it does not have works, is dead, being alone. Indeed, a man may say, You have faith, and I have works: show me your faith without your works, and I will show you my faith by my works" (James 2:17-18).

The believer's salvation is the perfect workmanship of God. Once a person receives the gift of perfect salvation, his life becomes a project in the hands of God. God's predetermined purpose for each believer is that the believer will be conformed to the character image of Jesus Christ. Paul reveals in Romans everything which God allows in a believer's life is working toward His purpose of developing the character of Christ in the believer. In order for the believer to understand what God wants to develop in his life, he must study the Scriptures to learn the character of Christ.

> And we know that all things work together for good to those who love God, to those who are the called according to his purpose. For whom he did foreknow, he also did predestinate *to be conformed to the image of his Son,* that he might be the firstborn among many brethren. (Romans 8:28-29)

Every workman begins with the raw materials necessary in his field of expertise. This discussion is about God's expertise in working with humans. In dealing with humans, there are vast differences in the raw material with which God must begin. The number of differences in humans is incalculable. Every human is totally unique.

Humans are different in physical appearance and physical ability, innate mental abilities, interests, emotional outlook, natural gifts, etc. Each human has had different life experiences, unique family interactions, dealt with differing circumstances, attained various levels of economic standing, etc. All this, and much more results in the person one has become at the time of his salvation.

The only raw material with which God has to work has been beaten, battered and broken by sin. By His grace, He saves and creates a new self within a believer. God then continues His craftsmanship by shaping and conforming the life of the believer, so the believer's life matches the new self.

One can be assured of one truth. God always has a plan. The believer may not be able to see nor discern God's plan for his life, but he must trust his Creator's plan. Too often believers forget God's plan is not about the temporal, but rather is about the eternal. His plan is about what is best for eternity. "And we know that all things work together for good to those who love God, to those who are the called according to his purpose" (Romans 8:28).

When one studies the intricacies of creation, he understands the all-wise Creator gave great attention to detail in His design and the implementation of His work. This same attention to detail is involved in the work God is doing in the life of a believer. In His wisdom, He directs or allows that which will produce what He desires to see in the life of the believer. He knows what works best for the raw material with which He is working. He has the wisdom to deal with every believer's uniqueness.

God has the skill to make what He desires to make. Just as a craftsman knows which tool to use for a specific task, God knows exactly what is needed to develop what He desires to see in the life of a believer. As the all-knowing God, He knows exactly what is needed for each believer.

God has made every believer a spiritual masterpiece of His grace in salvation. In His work on the believer after salvation, He seeks to produce a masterpiece life which brings forth good works glorifying God. Producing good works is to be the natural practice of those who are God's workmanship. God has made believers who they are and has determined they should produce good works because of who they are.

When a craftsman works to produce a masterpiece, the process is often very rough on the raw material with which he is working. The sculptor's chisel and hammer are very tough on the stone when he begins to chip away everything which is not part of his design. When a sculptor produces an image in or from the wood, his knife whittles away the unnecessary wood. The metal worker uses the anvil, heat and a hammer to produce his work.

When God is producing His masterpiece, things often get tough on His raw material. One of God's most noteworthy masterpieces is the Apostle Paul. Here is his testimony of some of the trials he had gone through in the process of becoming God's masterpiece.

> 23 Are they ministers of Christ? (I speak as a fool) I am more; in labors more abundant, in stripes above measure, in prisons more frequent, in deaths often.
> 24 From the Jews five times I received forty stripes save one.
> 25 Three times was I beaten with rods, once was I stoned, three times I was shipwrecked, a night and a day I have been in the deep;
> 26 In journeys often, in perils of waters, in perils of robbers, in perils by my own countrymen, in perils by the heathen, in perils in the city, in perils in the wilderness, in perils in the sea, in perils among false brethren;
> 27 In weariness and painfulness, in sleeplessness often, in hunger and thirst, without food often, in cold and nakedness. (II Corinthians 11:23-27)

Paul declares in Romans 8:28, "And we know that all things work together for good to those who love God, to those who are the called according to his purpose." He does not say all things are good. The believer must know and accept the reality all things whether he views them as good are as bad are working for the eternal good of those who love God.

The New Testament book of James instructs believers how to view trials of all kinds. Be assured all kinds of trials will come.

When the believer views trials properly, he will produce what God desires in his life. When a believer does not understand what God is trying to accomplish in his life, he can simply ask God for wisdom to know and understand. God will gladly give the wisdom needed.

> 2 My brethren, count it all joy when you fall into various trials;
> 3 Knowing this, that the testing of your faith produces patience.
> 4 But let patience have its perfect work, that you may be perfect and complete, lacking nothing.
> 5 If any of you lack wisdom, let him ask of God, who gives to all men liberally and does not criticize; and it shall be given to him. (James 1:2-5)

The Apostle Peter also addressed the necessity of trials in producing a praiseworthy faith. Those to whom he was writing were rejoicing with a glorious inexpressible joy in the midst of their trials.

> 6 In this you greatly rejoice, though now for a time, if need be, you are in heaviness through various trials
> 7 That the trial of your faith, being much more precious than of gold that perishes, though it is tried with fire, might be found unto praise and honor and glory at the appearing of Jesus Christ:
> 8 Whom having not seen, you love; in whom, though now you do not see him, yet believing, you rejoice with joy unspeakable and full of glory:
> 9 Having received the end of your faith, even the salvation of your souls. (I Peter 1:6-9)

Every believer is a glorious spiritual masterpiece created by the saving grace of the living God. God is still working on every believer to create a masterpiece life which makes His grace visible to this world. Things go much better when the believer learns to cooperate with God as He creates His masterpiece.

"Being confident of this very thing, that he who has begun a good work in you will continue it until the day of Jesus Christ (Philippians 1:6).

Colossians 3:12-17

12 Put on therefore, as the elect of God, holy and beloved, tender mercies, kindness, humility of mind, meekness, longsuffering;

13 Forbearing one another, and forgiving one another, if any man have a quarrel against another: even as Christ forgave you, so you must do also.

14 And above all these things put on love, which is the bond of perfection.

15 And let the peace of God rule in your hearts, to which you are also called in one body; and be thankful.

16 Let the word of Christ dwell in you richly in all wisdom; teaching and admonishing one another in psalms and hymns and spiritual songs, singing with grace in your hearts to the Lord.

17 And whatever you do in word or deed, do all in the name of the Lord Jesus, giving thanks to God and the Father by him. (KJBT)

Chapter 12
Made Near

> But now in Christ Jesus you who were far off **have been made near** by the blood of Christ.
> (Ephesians 2:13, KJBT)

The Apostle Paul is writing mainly to Gentiles in the book of Ephesians. In this verse he points to a pivotal turning point in their lives as believers. It is a statement contrasting the spiritual position in which they had previously been to the position which is now theirs in Christ. They had been far off from God, but now they had received the wonderful spiritual blessing of having been made near to Him. This critical change of position can only be achieved through the blood of Christ.

How far away from God had they been? In the verse just prior to this, Paul reminds them how far away they had been in their unsaved condition. "At that time you were without Christ, being aliens from the commonwealth of Israel, and strangers from the covenants of promise, having no hope, and without God in the world" (Ephesians 2:12). In this verse he itemizes five circumstances to demonstrate how far away from God they had previously been. The combination of these five things Paul enumerates reveals the terrible situation that had formerly existed for the Ephesians as Gentiles.

Paul first says they were "without Christ". This means they not only had no knowledge of Christ, but they were also without any way of coming to know Christ. As Gentiles they had no link to any revelation of a Messiah Savior who had come through the Jews. Previously, they were in the sad condition of being lost and completely unaware Christ existed.

Next, Paul notes as Gentiles they had been "aliens from the commonwealth of Israel." A commonwealth is a nation. The Gentiles had never been part of the nation of Israel. They had no heritage of what God had done in and through Israel as revealed in the Old Testament. None of their ancestors had been citizens of Israel. In their previous state, they had been absolute foreigners to what God had done through the seed of Abraham.

The third item in Paul's list is they had been "strangers from the covenants of promise." The Gentiles had no part in the promise of a redeeming Messiah. The promise was the unconditional promise which God gave to Abraham and reiterated in His covenant with David. As "strangers," the Gentiles were totally unaware of the promises to Abraham and his descendants.

The fourth circumstance in Paul's list reveals they had been in an awful situation of "no hope." Previously, they had been totally ignorant of the salvation which God provided. They were without any knowledge of the Christ in whom salvation could be found. They had been completely devoid of hope. They had absolutely nothing for which to hope beyond life in this world and could do nothing about it.

The fifth truth in Paul's list completes his description of their formerly grim situation. He says they had been "without God in this world." Though the Gentiles had worshipped many gods, they had no knowledge of the one true and living God who is revealed in the Scriptures. Though they were religious and committed in their worship of the gods of this world, they were "without God."

How far from God had the Gentiles been before coming to know Christ. Paul was not talking about a physical or geographic distance. He was talking about a spiritual distance. As one can see from Paul's list, they had been in a horrible and hopeless situation. Spiritually, there had been an infinite chasm of unbelief between them and God. It was a distance they could never traverse on their own. Because of their sin and rebellion, they had been destitute of holiness. They had been condemned and were under God's wrath. They had neither the capacity, nor the desire to commune with the living God.

"But now" (Ephesians 2:13) reveals a dramatic and drastic change in their position. They had gone from an infinite distance away from God to their new position in Christ of having been "made near" to God. This close proximity to the true and living God was provided by grace through the blood of Christ.

They had gone from being without any knowledge of Christ to understanding the mysteries of Christ. "To whom God chose to make known what are the riches of the glory of this mystery among the Gentiles; which is Christ in you, the hope of glory" (Colossians 1:27). In Christ they now knew and worshipped the true and living God.

They had now become citizens of the commonwealth of Israel to which they had previously been aliens. "Now therefore you are no longer strangers and foreigners, but fellow citizens with the saints, and of the household of God" (Ephesians 2:19). They had become members of God's family along with the believing Jews.

Having been "grafted" into Israel by faith, the Gentiles had now accessed the salvation promised in the covenants of Israel. "And if some of the branches are broken off, and you, being a wild olive tree, were grafted in among them, and with them partake of the root and fatness of the olive tree" (Romans 11:17). See Romans 11:11-25.

Now in Christ, the Gentiles had gone from having no hope to possessing the hope of glory. They now had an assured expectation of an eternal home beyond this world. They were now looking for the same city for which Abraham sought. "Now our Lord Jesus Christ himself, and God, even our Father, who has loved us, and has given us everlasting consolation and good hope through grace" (II Thessalonians 2:16).

As Gentiles they had gone from being without the true and living God to embracing Him and being embraced by Him. Now they could approach God. Now they had access to God in prayer with the assurance He would hear.

This dramatic and drastic change in the Gentiles was wrought by the grace of God. This grace was provided through the blood of Christ. Christ paid the price so their sin could be removed. The price Christ paid would have to be appropriated by faith. There was nothing which they could do to overcome their infinite spiritual distance from God. However, the infinite spiritual distance of separation from God was overcome when they by faith trusted in the blood of the infinite Christ for salvation.

This glorious change brought them near to God. How near to God were they? They were in Christ, and Christ was in them. "At that day you shall know that I am in my Father, and you in me, and I in you" (John 14:20).

Jews had been given many spiritual advantages which the Gentiles had not possessed. The Jews, however, had not taken advantage of what they had been given. The majority of the Jews rejected the Messiah who had been promised to them by divine revelation.

Paul points out Jews and Gentiles who trust in Christ are brought together as one. The division which had existed between them has now been abolished. Both are citizens of the same commonwealth and members of the same family. There is one body of which Christ is the Head. Jews and Gentiles "are built together for a habitation of God through the Spirit." This habitation of God is the Church.

14 For he is our peace, who has made both one, and has broken down the middle wall of partition between us;
15 Having abolished in his flesh the enmity, even the law of commandments contained in ordinances; in order to make in himself from two one new man, so making peace;
16 And that he might reconcile both unto God in one body by the cross, having slain the enmity by it:
17 And came and preached peace to you who were far off, and to those who were near.
18 For through him we both have access by one Spirit unto the Father.
19 Now therefore you are no longer strangers and foreigners, but fellow citizens with the saints, and of the household of God;
20 And are built upon the foundation of the apostles and prophets, Jesus Christ himself being the chief corner stone;
21 In whom all the building rightly framed together grows unto a holy temple in the Lord:
22 In whom you also *are built together for a habitation of God through the Spirit.*
(Ephesians 3:14-22)

Romans 5:1-11

1 Therefore, being justified by faith, we have peace with God through our Lord Jesus Christ:
2 By whom also we have access by faith into this grace in which we stand and rejoice in hope of the glory of God.
3 And not only so, but we glory in tribulations also: knowing that tribulation produces patience;
4 And patience, experience; and experience, hope:
5 And hope does not disappoint; because the love of God is shed abroad in our hearts by the Holy Spirit who is given unto us.
6 For when we were yet without strength, in due time Christ died for the ungodly.
7 For scarcely for a righteous man will one die: yet perhaps for a good man some would even dare to die.
8 But God demonstrated his love to us, in that, while we were yet sinners, Christ died for us.
9 Much more then, being now justified by his blood, we shall be saved from wrath through him.
10 For if, when we were enemies, we were reconciled to God by the death of his Son, much more, being reconciled, we shall be saved by his life.
11 And not only so, but we also joy in God through our Lord Jesus Christ, by whom we have now received the atonement. (KJBT)

Discussion Guide for Group Study

Introduction

1. What does it mean to have a vital union with Christ?
2. How may one have a vital union with Christ?

Chapter 1 – Redemption

1. Discuss your redemption experience.
2. Explain John 8:36 in your own experience.
3. How did Christ deliver believers from the bondage of the law?
4. How did Christ overcome the three aspects of death?

Chapter 2 – Forgiveness

1. What does it mean to you to be forgiven?
2. Discuss the various realities of forgiveness.
3. Explain the phrase, "our sin debt is Paid in Full."
4. Discuss the "riches of His grace."

Chapter 3 – Holy and Without Blame

1. Explain what it means to be "holy before Him."
2. Explain what it means to "without blame before Him."
3. How can one be "holy and without blame before Him"?
4. What is the focus of one who is "holy and without blame"?

Chapter 4 – Adoption

1. What does in mean to be adopted?
2. Why did God adopt believers?
3. How are God's adopted children to live in this world?
4. Discuss what God sees as best for His children.

Chapter 5 – Accepted

1. Why are humans rejected by God?
2. Discuss what humans do in their failed attempts to be accepted by God.
3. How may humans be accepted by God?
4. How does God view one who is in Christ?

Chapter 6 – An Inheritance

1. Discuss Peter's description of the believer's inheritance.
2. Discuss John's description of the believer's inheritance.
3. How does one "obtain an inheritance"?
4. Discuss the certainty of the believer's inheritance.

Chapter 7 – Sealed with the Holy Spirit

1. When is one sealed with the Holy Spirit?
2. Discuss the various aspects of a seal in relation to the Holy Spirit in a believer.
3. Discuss the Holy Spirit as the "down payment" on a believer's inheritance.
4. Discuss the phrase "Holy Spirit of promise."

Chapter 8 – Enlightened

1. How are one's spiritual eyes enlightened?
2. Why do humans need their spiritual eyes enlightened?
3. Discuss enlightenment in connection to wisdom and revelation.
4. Discuss the value of a believer to his Heavenly Father.

Chapter 9 – Empowered

1. What is the source of the believer's spiritual power?
2. Discuss and describe God's power.
3. Discuss the illustrations of God's power that Paul uses.
4. Discuss the reality that God's power is at work **in** and **for** the believer.

Chapter 10 – Spiritually Alive

1. Discuss Paul's description of being spiritually dead.
2. How are the spiritually dead "made alive"?
3. What motivated God to bring spiritually dead humans to life?
4. According to Peter, how spiritually dead are unsaved humans?

Chapter 11 – God's Workmanship

1. Discuss what the word workmanship means.
2. Discuss the process a workman uses to produce his masterpiece.
3. Discuss the two aspects of the masterpiece which God is producing.
4. What is God's raw material in producing His workmanship?

Chapter 12 – Made Near

1. How far from God had the Ephesians been before salvation?
2. Discuss what the words "but now" mean.
3. How near to God had the Ephesians been brought?
4. How had the Ephesians been made near?

About the King James Bible for Today

I was converted over fifty years ago. After being saved I was instructed by the pastor to read the Bible regularly. As a teenager I began to read the *Authorized King James Version* of the Bible faithfully. In the beginning it was extremely difficult. However, as I continued to read the Bible, I learned to change many of the words and word endings that are no longer in use today as I read. After a while changing the words became automatic as I read. I was then able to read and more clearly understand the Bible. I remember thinking back then as a teenager that someone needed to update the language in the Bible.

As I was celebrating my fiftieth spiritual birthday in June of 2014 I was thinking back to those days and the impact the *Authorized King James Bible* had on my life and ministry. It occurred to me that the English of the *Authorized King James Version* still has not been updated. Many new translations have been published since I was saved but no one has simply updated the English in the *Authorized King James Version*. So, I set out on a mission to do on paper what I learned to do in my head fifty years ago.

The *Authorized King James Version* has had several revisions since it was first printed in 1611. There were minor revisions with the printings between 1611 and 1616. The first major revision was in 1629 in which the Apocrypha was dropped. There were other major revisions in 1638 and 1762. The last major revision was in 1769. This 1769 revision is what has been called the *Authorized King James Version* ever since. There is a tremendous difference between the 1611 and the 1769 editions of the *Authorized King James Version* because 158 years had passed, and the English language had changed significantly. It has been over 250 years since that 1769 revision and the English language has changed tremendously in those 250+ years.

The *King James Bible for Today* is not a new translation. It simply updates the archaic words, spellings and endings of the old English into today's English. It does not alter the message of the *Authorized King James Version* but rather makes it easier to understand for today's Bible reader.

Ephesians - KJBT

1 Paul, an apostle of Jesus Christ by the will of God, to the saints who are at Ephesus, and to the faithful in Christ Jesus:

2 Grace be to you, and peace, from God our Father, and from the Lord Jesus Christ.

3 Blessed be the God and Father of our Lord Jesus Christ, who has blessed us with all spiritual blessings in heavenly places in Christ:

4 According as he has chosen us in him before the foundation of the world, that we should be holy and without blame before him in love:

5 Having predestinated us unto the adoption of children by Jesus Christ to himself, according to the good pleasure of his will,

6 To the praise of the glory of his grace, in which he has made us accepted in the beloved.

7 In whom we have redemption through his blood, the forgiveness of sins, according to the riches of his grace;

8 In which he has abounded toward us in all wisdom and prudence;

9 Having made known unto us the mystery of his will, according to his good pleasure which he has purposed in himself:

10 That in the dispensation of the fullness of times he might gather together in one all things in Christ, both which are in heaven, and which are on earth; even in him:

11 In whom we have also obtained an inheritance, being predestinated according to the purpose of him who works all things after the counsel of his own will:

12 That we who first trusted in Christ should be to the praise of his glory.

13 In whom you also trusted, after you heard the word of truth, the gospel of your salvation: in whom also after you believed, you were sealed with the Holy Spirit of promise,

14 Who is the down payment on our inheritance until the redemption of the purchased possession, unto the praise of his glory.

15 Therefore I also, after I heard of your faith in the Lord Jesus, and love unto all the saints,

16 Do not cease to give thanks for you, making mention of you in my prayers;

17 That the God of our Lord Jesus Christ, the Father of glory, may give unto you the spirit of wisdom and revelation in the knowledge of him:

18 The eyes of your understanding being enlightened; that you may know what the hope of his calling is, and what the riches of the glory of his inheritance in the saints,

19 And what the exceeding greatness of his power toward us who believe is, according to the working of his mighty power,

20 Which he worked in Christ, when he raised him from the dead, and set him at his own right hand in the heavenly places,

21 Far above all principality, and power, and might, and dominion, and every name that is named, not only in this world, but also in that which is to come:

22 And has put all things under his feet, and made him the head over all things to the church,
23 Which is his body, the fullness of him who fills all in all.

2
And he has made you alive, who were dead in trespasses and sins;
2 In time past you walked according to the course of this world, according to the prince of the power of the air, the spirit that now works in the children of disobedience:
3 Among whom we also all had our way of living in times past in the lusts of our flesh, fulfilling the desires of the flesh and of the mind; and were by nature the children of wrath, even as others.
4 But God, who is rich in mercy, for his great love with which he loved us,
5 Even when we were dead in sins, has made us alive together with Christ, (by grace you are saved;)
6 And has raised us up together, and made us sit together in heavenly places in Christ Jesus:
7 That in the ages to come he might show the exceeding riches of his grace in his kindness toward us through Christ Jesus.
8 For by grace are you saved through faith; and that not of yourselves: it is the gift of God:
9 Not of works, lest any man should boast.
10 For we are his workmanship, created in Christ Jesus unto good works, which God has before ordained that we should walk in them.
11 Therefore remember, that you being in time past Gentiles in the flesh, who are called uncircumcision by those who are called the circumcision in the flesh made by hands;
12 At that time you were without Christ, being aliens from the commonwealth of Israel, and strangers from the covenants of promise, having no hope, and without God in the world:
13 But now in Christ Jesus you who were far off have been made near by the blood of Christ.
14 For he is our peace, who has made both one, and has broken down the middle wall of partition between us;
15 Having abolished in his flesh the enmity, even the law of commandments contained in ordinances; in order to make in himself from two one new man, so making peace;
16 And that he might reconcile both unto God in one body by the cross, having slain the enmity by it:
17 And came and preached peace to you who were far off, and to those who were near.
18 For through him we both have access by one Spirit unto the Father.
19 Now therefore you are no longer strangers and foreigners, but fellow citizens with the saints, and of the household of God;
20 And are built upon the foundation of the apostles and prophets, Jesus Christ himself being the chief corner stone;
21 In whom all the building rightly framed together grows unto a holy temple in the Lord:
22 In whom you also are built together for a habitation of God through the Spirit.

3
For this reason I Paul, the prisoner of Jesus Christ for you Gentiles,

2 If you have heard of the dispensation of the grace of God which is given me toward you:
3 How that by revelation he made known unto me the mystery; (as I wrote before in few words,
4 By which, when you read, you may understand my knowledge in the mystery of Christ)
5 Which in other ages was not made known unto the sons of men, as it is now revealed unto his holy apostles and prophets by the Spirit;
6 That the Gentiles should be fellow heirs, and of the same body, and partakers of his promise in Christ by the gospel:
7 Of which I was made a minister, according to the gift of the grace of God given unto me by the effective working of his power.
8 Unto me, who is less than the least of all saints, is this grace given, that I should preach among the Gentiles the unsearchable riches of Christ;
9 And to make all men see what the fellowship of the mystery is, which from the beginning of the world has been hidden in God, who created all things by Jesus Christ:
10 To the intent that now unto the principalities and powers in heavenly places might be known by the church the manifold wisdom of God,
11 According to the eternal purpose which he carried out in Christ Jesus our Lord:
12 In whom we have boldness and access with confidence by the faith in him.
13 Therefore I ask you not to be discouraged by my tribulations for you, which is your glory.
14 For this cause I bow my knees unto the Father of our Lord Jesus Christ,
15 From whom the whole family in heaven and earth is named,
16 That he would grant you, according to the riches of his glory, to be strengthened with might by his Spirit in the inner man;
17 That Christ may dwell in your hearts by faith; that you, being rooted and grounded in love,
18 May be able to comprehend with all saints what is the breadth, and length, and depth, and height;
19 And to know the love of Christ, which passes knowledge, that you might be filled with all the fullness of God.
20 Now unto him who is able to do exceedingly abundantly above all that we ask or think, according to the power that works in us,
21 Unto him be glory in the church by Christ Jesus throughout all ages, world without end. Amen.

4 I therefore, the prisoner of the Lord, beseech you that you walk worthy of the calling to which you are called,
2 With all lowliness and meekness, with longsuffering, forbearing one another in love;
3 Endeavoring to keep the unity of the Spirit in the bond of peace.
4 There is one body, and one Spirit, even as you are called in one hope of your calling;
5 One Lord, one faith, one baptism,
6 One God and Father of all, who is above all, and through all, and in you all.
7 But unto every one of us is given grace according to the measure of the gift of Christ.

8 Therefore he said, When he ascended up on high, he led captivity captive, and gave gifts unto men.

9 (Now that he ascended, what is it but that he also descended first into the lower parts of the earth?

10 He who descended is also the same who ascended up far above all heavens, that he might fill all things.)

11 And he gave some, apostles; and some, prophets; and some, evangelists; and some, pastors and teachers;

12 For the perfecting of the saints, for the work of the ministry, for the edifying of the body of Christ:

13 Until we all come in the unity of the faith, and of the knowledge of the Son of God, unto a spiritually mature man, unto the measure of the stature of the fullness of Christ:

14 That from now on we no longer be children, tossed to and fro, and carried about with every wind of doctrine, by the trickery of men, and cunning craftiness, by which they lie in wait to deceive;

15 But speaking the truth in love, may grow up into him in all things, who is the head, even Christ:

16 From whom the whole body rightly joined together and held together by that which every joint supplies, according to the effective working of every part doing its job, makes the body grow unto the edifying of itself in love.

17 This I say therefore, and testify in the Lord, that from now on you do not walk as other Gentiles walk, in the futility of their mind,

18 Having the understanding darkened, being alienated from the life of God through the ignorance that is in them, because of the blindness of their heart:

19 Who being past feeling have given themselves over unto sensuality, to work all uncleanness with greediness.

20 But you have not so learned Christ;

21 If it be that you have heard him, and have been taught by him, as the truth is in Jesus:

22 That you put off concerning your former self the old man, which is corrupt according to the deceitful lusts;

23 And be renewed in the spirit of your mind;

24 And that you put on the new man, which after God is created in righteousness and true holiness.

25 Therefore putting away lying and speak every man truth with his neighbor: for we are members one of another.

26 Be angry and do not sin: do not let the sun go down upon your wrath:

27 Neither give opportunity to the devil.

28 Let him who stole steal no more: but rather let him labor, working with his hands the thing which is good, that he may have to give to him who is in need.

29 Let no corrupt communication proceed out of your mouth, but rather that which is good to the use of edifying, that it may minister grace unto the hearers.

30 And do not grieve the Holy Spirit of God, by whom you are sealed unto the day of redemption.

31 Let all bitterness, and wrath, and anger, and quarreling, and evil speaking, be put away from you, with all malice:

32 And be kind one to another, tenderhearted, forgiving one another, even as God for Christ's sake has forgiven you.

5 Therefore be imitators of God, as dear children;

2 And walk in love, as Christ also has loved us, and has given himself for us an offering and a sacrifice to God for a sweet smelling savor.
3 But sexual immorality, and all uncleanness, or covetousness, let in not once be named among you, as becomes saints;
4 Neither filthiness, nor foolish talking, nor jesting, which are not fitting: but rather giving of thanks.
5 For this you know, that no sexually immoral person, nor unclean person, nor covetous man, who is an idolater, has any inheritance in the kingdom of Christ and of God.
6 Let no man deceive you with empty words: for because of these things the wrath of God is coming upon the children of disobedience.
7 Therefore do not be partakers with them.
8 For once you were darkness, but now you are light in the Lord: walk as children of light:
9 (For the fruit of the Spirit is in all goodness and righteousness and truth)
10 Determine what is acceptable unto the Lord.
11 And have no fellowship with the unfruitful works of darkness, but rather expose them.
12 For it is a shame even to speak of those things which are done by them in secret.
13 But all things that are exposed are made clear by the light: for what exposes is light.
14 Therefore he said, Awake you who sleep, and arise from the dead, and Christ shall give you light.

15 See then that you walk looking around, not as fools, but as wise,
16 Making the best use of the time because the days are evil.
17 Therefore do not be unwise, but understanding what the will of the Lord is.
18 And do not be drunk with wine, which leads to riotous living; but be filled with the Spirit;
19 Speaking to yourselves in psalms and hymns and spiritual songs, singing and making melody in your heart to the Lord;
20 Giving thanks always for all things unto God and the Father in the name of our Lord Jesus Christ;
21 Submitting yourselves one to another in the fear of God.
22 Wives, submit yourselves unto your own husbands, as unto the Lord.
23 For the husband is the head of the wife, even as Christ is the head of the church: and he is the savior of the body.
24 Therefore, as the church is subject unto Christ, so let the wives be to their own husbands in everything.
25 Husbands, love your wives, even as Christ also loved the church, and gave himself for it;
26 That he might sanctify and cleanse it with the washing of water by the word,
27 That he might present it to himself a glorious church, not having spot, or wrinkle, or any such thing; but that it should be holy and without blemish.
28 Men should love their wives as their own bodies. He who loves his wife loves himself.
29 For no man ever yet hated his own flesh; but nourishes and cherishes it, even as the Lord the church:
30 For we are members of his body, of his flesh, and of his bones.

31 For this cause shall a man leave his father and mother, and shall be joined unto his wife, and the two shall be one flesh.

32 This is a great mystery: but I speak concerning Christ and the church.

33 Nevertheless let every one of you in particular love his wife even as himself; and the wife see that she respects her husband.

6 Children, obey your parents in the Lord: for this is right.

2 Honor your father and mother; (which is the first commandment with promise)

3 That it may be well with you and that you may live long on the earth.

4 And fathers do not provoke your children to wrath: but bring them up in the nurture and admonition of the Lord.

5 Servants, be obedient to those who are your masters according to the flesh, with fear and trembling, in sincerity of heart, as unto Christ;

6 Not with eye-service, as men pleasers; but as the servants of Christ, doing the will of God from the heart;

7 With good will doing service, as to the Lord, and not to men:

8 Knowing that whatever good thing any man does, the same he shall receive from the Lord, whether he is slave or free.

9 And masters, do the same things unto them, without threatening: knowing that your Master also is in heaven; neither is there respect of persons with him.

10 Finally, my brethren, be strong in the Lord, and in the power of his might.

11 Put on the whole armor of God that you may be able to stand against the schemes of the devil.

12 For we do not wrestle against flesh and blood, but against principalities, against powers, against the rulers of the darkness of this world, against spiritual wickedness in high places.

13 Therefore, take unto you the whole armor of God that you may be able to withstand in the evil day, and having done all, to stand.

14 Stand therefore, having your loins girded with truth, and having on the breastplate of righteousness;

15 And your feet shod with the preparation of the gospel of peace;

16 Above all, taking the shield of faith, with which you shall be able to quench all the fiery darts of the wicked one.

17 And take the helmet of salvation, and the sword of the Spirit, which is the word of God:

18 Praying always with all prayer and supplication in the Spirit, and being watchful with all perseverance and supplication for all saints;

19 And for me, that utterance may be given unto me, that I may open my mouth boldly, to make known the mystery of the gospel,

20 For which I am an ambassador in bonds: that in this I may speak boldly, as I ought to speak.

21 So you also may know my affairs, and how I do, Tychicus, a beloved brother and faithful minister in the Lord, shall make all things known to you:

22 Whom I have sent unto you for the same purpose, that you might know our affairs and that he might comfort your hearts.

23 Peace be to the brethren, and love with faith, from God the Father and the Lord Jesus Christ.

24 Grace be with all those who love our Lord Jesus Christ in sincerity. Amen.

www.ingramcontent.com/pod-product-compliance
Lightning Source LLC
Chambersburg PA
CBHW050440010526
44118CB00013B/1608